MW00460005

CATHOLICS AND PROTESTANTS

PETER J. KREEFT

Catholics and Protestants

WHAT CAN WE LEARN
FROM EACH OTHER?

IGNATIUS PRESS   SAN FRANCISCO

Unless otherwise indicated, Scripture quotations are from Revised Standard Version of the Bible—Second Catholic Edition (Ignatius Edition) copyright © 2006 National Council of the Churches of Christ in the United States of America. Used by permission. All rights reserved worldwide.

Art and cover design by Davin Carlson

© 2017 Ignatius Press, San Francisco
All rights reserved
ISBN 978-1-62164-101-8
Library of Congress Control Number 2015953758
Printed in the United States of America ⊗

*For Kevin Offner,
who persuaded me
to write this book*

Contents

Introduction

I will count this book a success if you the reader remember just two or three of my points five years later. Of how many books can you remember three of their points five years later?

This book does not have a scholarly style, outline, or length. Each chapter is short and makes a single, simple point. That is how we remember things: in points, not in outlines. Thus, we say, "Oh, I remember that point." We don't say, "Oh, I remember that outline." We put points together in outlines only *after* we see them. This book is only about seeing them. I set them out for you to see, and then arrange, if you wish, but above all to apply to your life. I am only the little boy who says, "Look!"

The topic invites this unusual approach because we cannot see much of the "big picture" that is God's providential design for the healing and reuniting of His Church. We do not understand how He is doing it, but we can see that He is doing something today that was never done before: Protestants and Catholics are sincerely loving and listening to each other. What will happen next? God only knows.

So I deliberately resisted the temptation to rearrange these separate "looks" in a more logical order, or even to be sure there was no overlapping of content between any two of them, as there usually is in separate pieces. Instead, I kept them in a random order because that was the order in which they occurred to me. Read them in any order you wish. They are independent, like islands, or angels.

I *could* have outlined them. I love outlines, and I fancy I am quite good at inventing them. The habit comes from reading Saint Thomas Aquinas a lot. In fact, it is almost an addiction. But I refused to do so—not out of laziness (though I *am* lazy) but out of charity, for you, the reader, for your greater delight and the points' greater power. Pascal's *Pensées* would have been spoiled if God had allowed him to live long enough to organize and outline them into a book, as he had planned. So God in His mercy struck him dead at a young age for our sakes. OK, God, I've learned my lesson: You don't have to kill me to make this book readable.

That's all I need to say. The best introductions are short. "Heeeere's Johnny!" was a classic.

∽

But I should say one thing about issues.

There are many issues that divide Protestants and Catholics. This book does not claim to resolve them. It is neither a complete book of Catholic apologetics (though it contains some key Catholic arguments) nor a complete manual for ecumenical reconciliation (though it contains some key arguments to the effect that the two sides are much more reconcilable than most people on both sides think). It is written from a point of view that is catholic (universal) as well as Catholic (Roman).

That catholicism with a small *c*, that universality, is one of the reasons I am a Roman Catholic. For I discovered more and more, the more I looked at the issues in the two thousand years of rich Church history, that the Catholic Church habitually sees both sides of every issue: e.g., God's oneness and threeness; Christ's divinity and humanity; predestination and free will; faith and works; Bible and Church; grace and nature; the absolute and eternal worth of the individual soul and the social priority of the common good. Whenever two positive things seem to conflict, the Church sorts them out as some kind of a "both-and" instead of a simple "either-or". The Church is in the marriage business with ideas as well as people. (That does not mean, of course, that negative ideas cannot disguise themselves as positive ones, or that heresies can easily be identified by their negative grammar.)

So here, right up front, is my master argument for Catholic thought: It is catholic. Catholics believe everything in the Bible, including the "Protestant" stuff. Lutherans may believe in Galatians versus James, faith versus works, but Catholics believe both. Calvinists may believe in predestination versus free will and Arminians in free will versus predestination, but Catholics, like Augustine and Aquinas, believe both. Whatever truths Protestantism teaches, Catholicism also teaches. Catholicism is inclusive, not exclusive. It does not like words like "merely" or "only" or *sola*. *Sola scriptura*, *sola fide*, and *sola gratia* were the three slogans of the Reformation—as if scripture excluded Tradition instead of presupposing it and referring to it and affirming it; and as if faith excluded works instead of necessarily producing the works of charity by its very essence, as mothers produce babies; and as if grace set aside nature and human nature rather than using and perfecting nature (and natural reason).

But those are apologetical arguments. This book is not about apologetics but about ecumenism.

Protestants may err by seeing too little in Catholicism, but I do not want to err by seeing too little in Protestantism. So I will perhaps surprise or even offend some Catholics by seeing what they may judge as too much truth in Protestantism. My defense is that I believe I can find it all in Catholicism. This is not an attempt to practice a kind of shuttle diplomacy or political compromise between two philosophies external to each other. I'm not importing some Protestant points into Catholicism. I'm just reminding Catholics and Protestants alike that these points are already there.

I

A Lutheran Parable

Sometimes truth can be best told by fiction. Parables are short fictions that tell important truths. I claim the following parable to be true.

In the year 1517 the Angel of God was sent to Germany to a passionate and pious Augustinian monk who had just discovered the essence of Christianity for the first time in his life and was on fire to share and spread this fire (not *his* fire, *Christ's* fire) in order to rekindle his brothers and sisters with it, since in many of them the fire looked tamped down, tamed, and tepid under the weight of its own massive and magnificent ecclesiastical fireplace.

"Brother Martin, you have been raised up by the all-seeing providence of God," said the Angel, "and given a great task. Though you are not the saint that Francis was, your divinely appointed task is the same task God gave to Francis three centuries ago when He said, 'My Church is in ruins; repair it.' Through the failures of your own life and the agonizing sufferings of your spirit, through the grace that brought you through them, He has shown you not just your needs but also what His Church needs today: nothing less than to rediscover her true strength and joy by rediscovering her own very foundation in the Gospel. You must remind her of this simple, liberating truth that you have discovered."

Brother Martin replied, "I joyfully accept this task. But how should I do this? What path shall I take?"

"You have a choice. There are three paths. The first path is made of ice, the second is made of fire, and the third is made of the love of Christ."

"I choose the third", Brother Martin said, instantly, with youthful passion.

"Ah, but it is not that easy", replied the angel. "The Devil stands very close behind you, unseen, to confuse you and to infiltrate his two false ways into the Way of Christ. I am here to warn you to beware and shun the two false ways. If you do not, then terrible things will come about, both in the Church and in the world, for many centuries. The Church will be torn asunder rather than repaired and reformed. Millions will be lost, and many will be deceived and in darkness."

"Do you tell me of the end of the world?"

"Death is the end of the world for each one of you. I speak of the world of human souls, not the world of stars and starfish. Do you think the Lord deigns to satisfy your curiosity about the time of the end for stars and starfish?"

"What are these two false paths, then? What is the path of ice?"

"It is the path many have already taken, as you already see: the freezing and starving of souls in their own beautiful House, the House built by God Himself to be their House of Bread. If they do not rekindle the fire in the hearth at the center of their House, the House of Bread will become as lifeless as a mausoleum. It will be the tomb of God, as a great prophet of the Antichrist, a man named Nietzsche, will prophesy. God has raised you up (and you are not the only one) to remind the housekeepers of this danger."

"I will remind them!" said Brother Martin, with sincere and simple passion.

"But it will not be easy. You will be tempted by the way of fire."

"I do not fear the fire of martyrdom."

"But there are subtler temptations on this way of fire."

"What do you mean?"

"I mean the fire of anger and pride. That is always the greatest of temptations. You nearly succumbed to despair for most of your life; now your temptation will be the opposite. And if you succumb to that temptation, that would make you resemble your enemies, both your enemies from Hell and your evil enemies within the Church. You will be tempted to self-righteousness even in preaching against self-righteousness. If you succumb to this temptation, that fire will destroy many souls and bodies. For many centuries Christians will consign each other's souls to Hell and each other's bodies to battlefield graves. The Church, which took over a thousand years to win the world, will lose it in half that time. Men will no longer say of Christians, 'See how they love one another', and run to them with love and envy, but they will say, 'See how they hate one another', and run away from them with disgust. Religious wars will rage and ruin religion."

"And what is the Way of Christ that avoids both these terrible false ways?"

"It is the way of divine love, the love that moves the Trinity forever, the love that moves the sun and the other stars, the love that moved Him to empty Himself of all twelve pints of His blood to save all twelve tribes of His children. That river of love is your path, and if you step out of that river, you will enter either the river of ice or the river of fire."

"I accept this task and this warning. Tell me, if you know: will I succeed?"

"I will not tell you yes or no, but I will tell you this: Even if you fail, the Lord will still use you to work out His plan, as He used even the rebellions and captivities of His chosen people Israel. But in that case the way will be long and hard and dark, and many will fall by the wayside."

"Should I tell the world of your words?"

"Tell no one of this vision. Remind yourself of it every day. The future of both the Church and the world is at stake."

The angel departed from Brother Martin, and the Devil immediately slipped into the empty place where the angel had been. And Martin took up an inkwell and cast it at the Devil, who retreated in haste. And then Martin took up his pen and ink and began to write, with piety and passion.

But as he retreated, the Devil had a small smile on his face.

2

Why the Reformation Is Over

Most Christians, Protestants as well as Catholics, do not know that the majority of Lutherans in the world seek *and expect* the Reformation to end and reunion with Rome to succeed some day. For that was Luther's original intention: reform, not revolt.

Most other Christians also have never even heard of the news of the greatest ecumenical achievement in the five hundred years since the Reformation, a truly miraculous achievement, which almost no one thought was possible. It is the Decree of Justification.[1] The single greatest obstacle to reunion, by far the most important religious difference between Protestants and Catholics, has essentially been overcome. Goliath is slain; it remains only to slay the other, smaller Philistines. There are many of them, but none are as big as Goliath.

No one saw this coming. The one notable exception was Hans Urs von Balthasar, in his doctoral thesis, written in the fifties, which claimed that there was no real contradiction between the quintessentially Catholic teaching of

[1] The complete text for the Decree of Justification may be found at the Vatican web site (http://www.vatican.va).

Saint Thomas Aquinas and the quintessentially Protestant Lutheran teaching of Karl Barth on the centrally divisive issue of justification.

Who is this Goliath? Ask any Evangelical what justified Luther's divorce with Rome, and he will say: the Gospel, the Good News that we are justified by faith in Christ, not by the works of the law. What justified Luther's break, they will say, was nothing less than the fact that Catholics, like the Galatians, had turned to "another gospel". They didn't know how to get to Heaven! They thought you had to buy your way in with enough good works. (And how many would be enough? Would 600 get you to Heaven but 599 to Hell?) In other words, "justification by faith" was the watchword of the Reformation. There are other issues too, but that one was the "biggie".

And it seems impossible to mediate the difference here between Protestantism and Catholicism. It seems logically impossible because either we are justified by faith alone, or faith alone is not enough and we also need good works. There is no logical possibility of compromise here; that would be like a compromise between the number one and the number two. It also seems ecclesiastically impossible because the Church officially condemned Luther's doctrine of justification by faith alone as a heresy, and Luther did the same to the Church's teaching on this issue. And reunion can never happen by compromise of truth, because truth is an absolute.

Well, the biggest obstacle to reunion has been overcome. Solved. Conquered. What couldn't be mediated without compromise has been mediated without compromise. It looked impossible, but "with God all things are possible" (Mt 19:26). Didn't you hear the news? Catholics and Lutherans (and many other Protestants who also came on board) have agreed that they don't really disagree, at least in substance, in essence, on justification, though they certainly seem to disagree in words. The Decree on Justification was ratified by the Vatican and the world's Lutherans at the highest official levels, in three stages, beginning in the 1990s.

How did this happen? By both sides going backward instead of forward. Instead of more details, more arguments, more justifications, more branches branching out in opposite directions and more of a load of leaves on each branch, both sides went back to their common trunk. What did all Christians believe in the beginning? What did the Apostles believe?

To answer that question, if we go back to our earliest data, the New Testament, we find that that foundational text itself seems to contradict itself. Galatians and Romans say we are justified by faith, not by the works of the law. But 1 Corinthians 13 and James say we need love (which in the Bible means not a feeling but the *works* of love,[2] freely chosen) and *not* faith alone. In fact, the words "faith alone" are indeed in the Bible when the Bible talks about "justification" (salvation), but they are not affirmed but denied: "A man is justified by works and *not* by faith alone" (Jas 2:24; emphasis added).

What did Christians do about this apparent contradiction in their data? For a while, Luther took the easy way out and simply denied that James belonged in the canon of the Bible. But he later repented of this arrogant mis-

---

[2] *Works of Love* is the title of a book written by the greatest Protestant philosopher of all time, Søren Kierkegaard—a Lutheran, no less. Its main point is that for Christianity love *is* the works of love.

take ("It can't be divine revelation because it disagrees with me!").

What Christians did about it was to fight religious wars about it for centuries. (War is the brilliant idea that the solution to disagreements is to kill each other.) Even when the physical wars quieted down in the twentieth century everywhere except in Northern Ireland, the verbal wars did not —until finally, a miracle happened: Protestants and Catholics came to agreement on justification, agreement without compromise, because they began to listen to each other, and to the scriptural data, and began to listen to each other's listening to the data.

The scriptural data are not as clear as both sides had typically made it out to be in past polemics. Peter, in fact, candidly calls the writings of Paul difficult and hard to understand (2 Pet 3:15–16). But like hunters, both sides, Protestant and Catholic, explored anew the difficulties, the darkest thickets of the problem, because that is where the most delicious game usually hides. It is the "hard sayings" that are the most important for us because they tell us things we do not yet understand. (That is why they're "hard"!)

To oversimplify the answer (oversimplifying is a necessity sometimes, as in a road map), Paul in Galatians and Romans used "justification" in a narrow sense (getting to Heaven, being saved) and "faith" in a broad sense (choosing to let Christ into your soul) when he said we are justified by faith, not by good works. The thief on the cross had no time for good works, but he was saved. ("Truly, I say to you, today you will be with me in Paradise" [Lk 23:43].) But James used "justification" in a broader sense: becoming totally reconciled to God, conformed to God, becoming what God demands, which includes sanctification, being made a perfect saint, as well as "getting saved". And he used "faith" in a narrower sense, as intellectual *belief*. Thus, he wrote, "Do you believe (have faith) that there is one God? Oooh, good for you! The devils also believe, and tremble" (Jas 2:19 —I like that translation; you can hear the sarcasm).[3] Paul uses "faith" in this narrower sense too sometimes, e.g., in 1 Corinthians 13, where he says we need not faith alone but also hope and charity (Christian love, which, remember, is the works of love), and in fact the greatest of these virtues is not faith but charity.

At the time of the Reformation debates, Protestants used Paul's language (in Romans and Galatians) and Catholics used James' language; and they were really talking past each other although they seemed to themselves to be talking to each other and contradicting each other. But you can't contradict each other unless you talk to each other. And you can't talk to each other and respond to each other unless you first listen to each other and speak the same language. What happened in our day that never happened before was that both sides listened with a new openness and passion and honesty, and the result was a miracle: the central issue of the Reformation, which was the single most serious schism in Christian history, was resolved to the satisfaction of both sides without compromise. That is why George Marsden said that "the Reformation is over."

Well, not quite. There are other issues, notably the teaching authority of the Church, which is behind all the teachings Catholics believe and Protestants don't because they don't find them clearly in the Bible (teachings like the Mass,

---

[3] The actual passage reads, "You believe that God is one; you do well. Even the demons believe—and shudder."

transubstantiation, the papacy, Marian doctrines, Purgatory, and prayers to saints). The overall issue is the relation between the Church and the Bible: is divine authority, for the Christian, supposed to be *sola scriptura* (scripture alone), as Luther said? Or does the Church and her Sacred Tradition handed down from Christ and the Apostles also have authority, and even, in some circumscribed circumstances, infallibility? Is her "Magisterium" (teaching authority) divine or only human? None of those issues has been resolved yet to the extent that the issue of justification has. But we're working on them! (And by "we" I mean not just Protestants-and-Catholics but also us-and-the-Holy-Spirit.)

But these issues *can* in principle be resolved in the same way as the justification issue was resolved: by mutual listening that is passionately honest, open, fair, charitable, receptive, eager, and faithful. The big iron wall between us is down; the other little wooden fences can come down too.

How? When? God only knows.

3

How Catholics Should
Think about Protestants

The answer to that question is obvious. They are Christ's brothers and ours. They are God's children. They are deeply loved. They are Christians. They are family members; they are deeply united with us even if they are *imperfectly* united with us.

What is not so obvious is how Catholics should think about Protestant*ism*, about its existence, about the Reformation. Apparently, it was not only a heresy but a tragedy. It split the Church. It produced terrible religious wars and was thus largely responsible for the fact that ever since the Reformation, Western civilization has become more anti-Christian.

Yet there is another side to the providential story that is equally true but less obvious: without Protestantism, there would have been no Council of Trent and no Vatican II. These are the two biggest and best reforming councils in modern times. And without them, where would the Church be?

Trent was a response to valid Protestant criticisms about not only particular corruptions like the sale of indulgences but, more generally, to the Church's lethargy, Pharisaical self-satisfaction, and apparent old-age sclerosis. Because of Trent, the Church showed new life and new power.

Vatican II was like a tide, moving the Church in a new direction: toward simplicity, toward human persons, and toward Christ Himself. And to do that, the Church used the same method in Vatican II as in the Decree on Justification. The technical, scholarly word for that method is *ressourcement*, a recapturing of her identity by returning to her first sources. Without denying her long and glorious (though spotted) history, the Church returned her focus and attention to her two primary sources, Christ and scripture; the Word of God on paper and the Word of God on wood (the Cross); the Word of God in the Spirit (scripture is "the sword of the spirit" [Eph 6:17]) and the Word of God in the flesh.

It had been Reformation Protestants who had first insisted on this return to the sources. So Catholics should thank God for prodding the Church in the right direction through these "heretics".

That does not mean giving up on any Catholic dogma. It means entering into the dogmas' essence, heart, and center. At that center we always find a Person. In fact, three Persons. Please reread the introduction to C.S. Lewis' *Mere Christianity* on that. (That simple, unscholarly little book probably did more for ecumenism than any other ever written.)

4

How *Not* to Think about Reunion

"Of course it would be nice if we all agreed, but we just don't, and can't."

There are five lies in that little sentence.

First, it is not an "of course". Most partisans enjoy fighting their civil wars.

Second, it is not a "would be". It is a "will be". When Christ comes back, He will marry the Church, not the churches. He will not marry a harem. The lacerations in His Body will be healed.

Third, we *do* agree—on Christ as our Lord; and that is the only basis for our future agreement on everything else that comes from His mind and will. Our already-present agreement is the most important thing because it is the basis for all our future agreements.

Fourth, we *can*. "Ought" implies "can" (you're not responsible for something that can't be done), and unity is a "can" because it is a solemn "ought". (If you doubt that, just read John 17, 1 Corinthians 1–2, and Saint John Paul II's encyclical *Ut Unum Sint*, the most ecumenical Church document in history.)

Finally, it is not "nice", it is necessary. It is a solemn, thunder-and-lightning-tinged order from Almighty God.

Here is absolute proof of this last point. What does God think of our divisions? Find out. How? It's easy. He told us. Read His Book. Read—and pray, if you dare—John 17:11, 21–23, and pray about 1 Corinthians 1:10–13, not just because I say so, not to find out what I think, but to find out what God thinks and says about the whole point of this book. Read these passages éven though you may have read them many times before. Read them as prayer, as part of your personal conversation with God, face-to-Face, in His presence. That can be deeply disconcerting and discombobulating if you dare to let Him speak to you, personally, here and now, instead of looking at His Book as if it is an impersonal letter generically addressed to "Dear Occupant". If you do that, it will put a duck into the Lord's Prayer: it will make you duck after you pray "Thy will be done."

Do it. Actually do it—now, before you read another paragraph. Don't just think about it—do it. "Yes, I agree; it is good to do it." Then do it, for God's sake. (I speak literally, not frivolously.) Put this book down and read *the* Book first. Reread Christ's prayer in John 17 and hear not just the concepts but the passion. Reread 1 Corinthians 1 and hear Paul's passion. See whether he has any tolerance at all for denominationalism. Then read Psalm 133:1; Romans 15:5–7; 2 Corinthians 13:11; Ephesians 3:1–14; Philippians 1:27; 2:2, 5; 4:2; and 1 Peter 3:8; 4:1. And if you don't have a Bible, go steal one.

Are you done? Welcome back. But you are *not* welcome back if you were too busy or impatient actually to do it, if you didn't have the courage to stop your mental flywheel that was so heavy with momentum. I will give you one more chance. If you don't think you have the time to listen to the Mind of Christ, the Word of God in person, as He expressed it to you through the Bible, the Word of God in words, then you're a very bad listener. It is bad enough to be a bad listener to man, but much worse to be a bad listener to God.

Assuming you took advantage of the second chance I gave you with this insult, welcome back. Now you know how God feels about this issue. So now you are in the right frame of mind—God's frame of mind—to read the rest of this book.

Your fishing trip into the Bible ended with a big fish on your hook, if you used the right fishing equipment: the hook of honest truth-seeking and the untangled line of simplicity and the sinker of humility and the worm of open-mindedness. You found the fish, you found the answer to the question: How important is this issue to God? It is non-negotiable because it is God's demand. It's as simple as that.

Ecumenical reunion is like the "social gospel", the creeds, baptism, or ministering to the poor: it is an ineradicable part of the whole Gospel. It is not the whole of the Gospel, and it is not the very center of it, but it is not an addition to it either. This thing is inextricably glued to the center of the Gospel, because the center of the Gospel is Christ Himself, and this thing is Christ's will and demand. So it is not an addition, like an outfit to wear at will, but it is like a limb or an organ of the body. You can take your clothes off, but you can't take your body off. Similarly, you can remove any of Christianity's historically relative aspects, such as its medieval political powers, but you can't remove any part of its essence. And unity in the Faith is as much a part of the essence of the Christian faith as the biological unity of an organic body is part of its essence.

And that unity in the Faith is both visible and invisible, as is the unity of a physical organism. Whether we are speaking of the natural organism of your body or of the supernatural organism of Christ's Body, whether we are speaking of the visible, material, biological body whose life is your soul, your spirit, or of the mystical Body whose soul is the Holy Spirit, the unity of that body is invisible because the unity of that body is not itself a body (unity has no color or mass) but rather is the life or "life force" or "soul" *of* that body. But it is also visible for the very same reason: because it is the life *of that visible body*, both in the case of your biological body and in the case of the visible historical Body of Christ that is the Church. When Saint Paul says we are "members" of that body, the word for "members" means literal organs, like hands or eyes or spleens. (Saint Jerome, e.g., was a spleen.)

This visible-and-invisible unity is ineradicably connected to the center of the Gospel (which is Christ Himself) for two reasons: first, because it is *Christ's* demand; and second, because it is *Christ's* mystical (yet visible) Body on earth that has these broken limbs that have to be healed and made whole.

It's nonnegotiable. We *have* to do it; we *have* to let ourselves be used as God's instruments to heal His own broken mystical Body. We have to be Churchillian bulldogs: "Never, never, never, never, never give in." It is not an ideal—it is a command.

5

What Happens in
Individuals Who "Ecumenize"?

Individuals who ecumenize don't just enter into polite ecumenical discussions, though they do that too. They don't just love each other and listen to each other, though they do that too. They don't just pray for each other and with each other, though they do that too. They discover something big and new.

Catholics discover the fire, and Protestants discover the fireplace. Catholics discover the essence of Evangelical Protestantism; a personal relationship with Jesus Christ as Lord and Savior. Protestants discover the essence of Catholicism; Christ's own visible, tangible Body, both as a living institution with teaching authority and as a real literal personal presence in the Eucharist.

It is not that these two things are totally missing on either side. Yet when Catholics and Protestants meet each other on the deep level of religious faith, this is what very often happens, because most Catholics have minimized the fire and most Protestants have minimized the fireplace.

In this meeting, both parties change by addition, not by subtraction. No one gives up anything. Both add rather than subtract. Or rather, both recover what they used to have together, in the time of the Apostles and the martyrs and the catacombs and again in the time of the medieval saints and mystics and cathedral builders. If it was possible then, it is possible again!

I like to call this the "math of more". There is no "less". It is not like taking some dollars away from one pocket to fill the other pocket. It is not even like taking the same number of dollars out of each pocket to fill the other pocket. It is like sex, not like money: men become more masculine, not less, and women become more feminine, not less, when they meet and mix. When they give themselves to each other they do not lose themselves but gain themselves. The same is true of every kind of human love: friendship, affection, and charity as well as romance. Protestant-Catholic ecumenism is like Jewish-Christian ecumenism in that way: Christians become more Christian by becoming more Jewish, and Jews become more Jewish by becoming Christian. Christians rediscover their own forgotten Jewish roots (Pope Pius XI said that "spiritually, we [all Christians] are Semites"),[1] and Jews discover the fullness of their own Judaism in the Messiah. They do not call themselves "ex-Jews" but "completed Jews". No one loses; everyone gains. In a parallel way, Catholics discover in Evangelical Protestantism[2] the very heart of Catholicism, what it is all about;

---

[1] Address to Belgian pilgrims, September 6, 1938, in *La documentation catholique* 29 (1938), col. 1460, quoted in "We Remember: A Reflection on the Shoah", by Commission for Religious Relations with the Jews, March 16, 1998, Holy See website, www.vatican.va.

[2] Throughout this book I speak only of Evangelical (in the broad sense) Protestantism, i.e., the Protestantism of the Reformers, not of liberal or modernist Protestantism, which is simply shrinkage and hopeless heresy.

and Evangelicals discover in Catholicism the fullest possible personal relationship to Christ, which is the essence of Evangelicalism. They fulfill themselves in each other, like man and woman.

That doesn't always happen. But it should. And it can, because sometimes it does.

6

The Greatest Confession of Failure in Church History

Only a few years ago, I had a shocking realization when thinking in the usual abstract, dull, and dreamy way about the phrase that the Church, following her last three popes, is using lately, that is, the "new evangelization". I suddenly realized that this is just not at all the nice, safe, comforting, sleepy-time PR slogan it seems to be. *This is the greatest confession of failure in Church history!*

Why? Because what is new in the "new evangelization" is not a new "evangel", a new gospel, but a new "ization". And by far the most important new feature of this new "ization" is not new technological means and media but a new audience. The Church is saying nothing less than this:

That the new mission field, the new paganism, the new "darkest Africa", is the members of the Catholic Church in the civilization that used to be called "Christendom".

That many, perhaps even most, of her members, at least in that old civilization, have been sacramentalized without being evangelized.

That she has failed to teach Lesson One.

That many Catholics don't even know how to be saved, how to get to Heaven.

That we Catholics have to go hat in hand to Protestant Evangelical heretics and learn from them what the essence of our own religion is.

That the Church that God appointed to be His prophet to the world today, after nearly two thousand years, is as spectacularly unsuccessful as were the People that God had chosen and appointed to be His collective prophet to the world two thousand years ago in Christ's day.

Oops.

(That is the new, streamlined Short Act of Contrition.)

It is not an accident that one of the most vibrant missionary societies, the Fellowship of Catholic University Students (FOCUS), is training missionaries to the new "darkest Africa". (In fact, many of these missionaries to America are from Africa; Christianity is growing, in both numbers and piety, more in Africa than anywhere else on earth.) The new "darkest Africa" is *Catholic college campuses*. That is where FOCUS missionaries go, because missionaries always go to the darkest spiritual ghettos, if they are allowed there. They are not yet allowed on any Jesuit campuses, which are usually the most pluralistic and tolerant of all other religions.

This is not a joke.

The second-largest Christian group in America, according to a Pew Research poll, is ex-Catholics. The largest group is Catholics. These are the two main mission fields for the Catholic Church's "new evangelization" today. The main reason there are so many ex-Catholics is that they never discovered Jesus Christ in the Catholic Church. If they had, they would never have left.

Protestants need to learn Lessons Two through Twenty-Two from us, but we need to learn Lesson One from them.

How dare Catholics look at the essence of Evangelicalism

—a personal relationship of faith, hope, and love with Jesus Christ as Lord and Savior—as an import, from a foreign religion into their own? That objection could only possibly be raised by those Catholics who do not know the very essence, center, and foundation of their own religion, of Christianity itself.

Anti-Catholic Protestants who still wonder whether Catholics are even Christians often contrast Catholicism and Christianity as an either-or. ("Are you a Catholic or are you a Christian?") Amazingly, many Catholics do the same! They use the word "Christians" to mean Evangelical Protestants.

Let me tell you about the greatest trauma in my teaching life. I often give my students a questionnaire at the beginning of a philosophy course to get to know them better. I ask them about their choices in books, movies, sports, music, morality, and religion ("How do you identify yourself religiously?"). Then I add this question: If you were to die tonight and meet God, and God asked you why He should let you into Heaven, what would you answer Him?

I classify their answers into three categories. The first answer is the Pharisaical answer: "I'm a good person", "I've done my best", "I've tried to be kind", "I've obeyed Your commandments", "I am compassionate and not judgmental", etc. These are always the most numerous, even among the students who identify themselves as Catholics! Pharisees today speak the language of pop psychology rather than the language of moral legalism, so they are disguised and rarely recognized as Pharisees; but they are at least as numerous and as influential as they were in Jesus' day. Technically, their heresy is called Pelagianism. It is self-salvation. You make yourself good enough to deserve Heaven.

The second answer is better, and humbler. It begins with a different pronoun, "You" instead of "I". It is hope in God's mercy, compassion, and love. That is good, of course, but it does not distinguish itself from Judaism or Islam. (The Qur'an mentions Allah's mercy seventeen times as often as His justice. I'll bet you didn't know that.)

The third answer, of course, is Jesus Christ. Nearly all students who label themselves as Evangelicals give it. Nearly all Catholic students do not. The number always runs between 0 and 5 percent. Can you possibly imagine a greater scandal in "Catholic education" than that? The most educated Catholics in America don't even know how to get to Heaven! That is like the most educated mathematicians in America not knowing the multiplication table.

But even though most of the Catholics here in the People's Republic of Massachusetts don't know it, Catholicism already has within it, at its very heart and center, the essence of Evangelicalism, a personal relationship with Christ. This was very clear from the beginning, throughout the New Testament and in all the Fathers of the Church and in all the saints and all the popes, and remains clear also in modern popular Catholic devotions such as Eucharistic adoration (who do you think that *is* there whom we adore, anyway?), and devotion to the Sacred Heart, and the Precious Blood, and the Holy Name, and Mary. *Whose* heart, *whose* blood, *whose* name? *Whose* Mother is Mary?

7

Catholic versus Protestant Perspectives on Tradition and Scripture

The difference between Catholics and Protestants on scripture can't be reduced to *sola scriptura* versus "scripture plus Tradition". That is an outside way of looking at it. There is also an inside way of looking at it—and that change of perspective changes everything you see. It is like when you start standing on your head, or when you stop standing on your head, which is what you do when you read G. K. Chesterton.

From the Catholic point of view, scripture *is part of* Tradition. Tradition is the whole of public authoritative teaching that comes from Christ through His Apostles and the Church that He and they planted.

When it comes to scripture, Protestants tend to split into fundamentalists versus modernists, or, more generally, conservatives versus liberals. In conservatives there tends to be an uneasiness about how scripture came about, by historical events that are human and temporal. The uneasiness arises from the knowledge that the effect (scriptural infallibility) seems to exceed its historical causes. Of course, the answer is that the Holy Spirit and divine providence *used* these fallible human causes to produce an infallible, divine effect. But

still, Bible-believing Protestants who tend to fundamentalism more than to modernism often treat the Bible as if it
originated in the same way Muslims say the Qur'an did: by
an immediate, direct, word-for-word once-for-all revelation
from an angel.

Fundamentalists are like Docetists, while modernists are
like Arians. (Docetism was the heresy that denied Christ's
humanity, and Arianism was the heresy that denied Christ's
divinity.) Fundamentalism denies, or at least downplays or
ignores, the Bible's humanity (thus, it is suspicious of the
"historical-critical method"), and modernism denies or de-
flates its divinity. The parallel between these two errors
about scripture (fundamentalism and modernism) and the
two errors about Christ (Docetism and Arianism) is appropriate because scripture itself uses the very same title—the
"Word of God"—both for itself and for Christ.

It is simply a historical fact that the Bible came about from
the practice of the living Church, handed down by Tradition. For (1) the Apostles created (wrote) scripture, (2) the
whole Church used it consistently,[1] and (3) the bishops of
the world, in union with the Bishop of Rome (the pope),
finally officially, authoritatively, and infallibly defined the
canon (list of books) in it, at the Council of Orange in the
fifth century. Yes, "infallibly". If that Church decision wasn't
infallible, then it is a matter of doubt whether perhaps the
Gnostic Gospel of Thomas belongs in scripture instead of

---

[1] Consistent use by the Church (in other words. her ongoing, uni-
form Tradition) was in fact the first standard the Church used to determine which books belonged in the canon of the New Testament.
That was the same kind of standard the Jews had used to determine
which books belonged in their canon, which Christians call the Old
Testament.

John's anti-Gnostic Gospel and letters. If the Bible is your only certainty, you can't be certain you have the right Bible, because the Bible doesn't include its own table of contents!

But if the effect cannot exceed the cause, how can a merely fallible Church produce or define an infallible scripture?

Is there any evidence that any of the Church Fathers thought that the Church was infallible *only* when defining the canon of scripture, and not in interpreting it in the creeds? No. None whatsoever.

It is a package deal: either both scripture and authoritative apostolic Tradition are infallible, or neither is. Each appeals to and depends on the other. They're like husband and wife. The issue that divides Catholics and Protestants about scripture is *not* "Are there two separate sources of revelation or one?" Neither one is separate from the other. The Bible is part of the Church's Sacred Tradition, and the Church and her Tradition are part of (pointed to by, included in, and authorized by) the Bible.

The Bible appeals to the authority of Tradition and Tradition appeals to the authority of the Bible. The Bible calls the *Church* "the pillar and bulwark of the truth" (1 Timothy 3:15), and the Church calls the Bible infallible divine revelation.

The Bible tells us that Christ authored and authorized the teaching authority of the Church, in the Apostles. History tells us that the Church (the Apostles) authored the Bible and that the Church (the bishops) later authorized (canonized, defined) it. The Church was the efficient cause (the producer) and the formal cause (the definer) of the Bible. The causal chain connects the Bible with Christ only through the Church. And a chain is only as strong as its weakest link.

The actual history of Protestantism shows a massive and natural slide toward modernism and liberalism and relativism and historicism concerning scripture. Nearly every mainline Protestant denomination has moved in that direction. There have been many modernist theologians in the Catholic Church too, but they are clearly defined as wrong by the official Magisterium, the rock of Peter that stands up against the floods of heresies. That rock does not exist outside of Rome. It is the only dike against the ocean of relativism that never springs leaks. Never has, never will.

The difference between seeing scripture as part of a larger thing (Sacred Tradition, the "deposit of faith") and seeing it alone is a difference in perspective, a difference in the frame rather than in the picture. The Catholic scripture, which is part of a full, living Sacred Tradition, and the Protestant *scriptura*, which is *sola* (alone), are the same scripture. But it is appreciated differently, and interpreted differently, and used differently because of the different frame, or perspective. There is a great difference between a poster of *The Last Supper* without a frame, and the same picture in a serious, heavy, golden frame that shouts in every molecule, "This is sacred!"

So if a Protestant really cares about scriptural infallibility and authority, he will embrace the Church as its strongest guarantor. And if a Catholic really cares about his Church's Tradition, he will listen to Saint Jerome, who says, "Ignorance of scripture is ignorance of Christ."

(See also chapter 32 for a longer reflection on the question of scripture and its relation to Tradition.)

8

Coming Home:
A Protestant-Catholic Dialogue

Here is how the dialogue typically goes, when both sides are strong:

CATHOLIC: Come home, my Protestant brother, come back to the Church you left five hundred years ago. We are the original Church; we are your family. You ran away from home. Come back.

PROTESTANT: We did not run from home. We ran from rottenness.

CATHOLIC: Yes. And so did we, later, at the Council of Trent. But we rejected the rottenness without rejecting the tree. You saw the tree of the Church as so rotten that you thought you had to break off a branch and plant it in pure soil. But you can't do that. The Church is Christ's visible Body, and you broke it.

PROTESTANT: No, we did not break it—you did. We left you in 1517 not because we wanted something new but because we wanted something old. *You* are the new kids on the block, the heretics. Your Catholic additions are heresies, and they accumulated like barnacles on the smooth, pure hull of the

40

ark, the early Church, until the Reformers scraped them off.

CATHOLIC: What you say are barnacles are in fact leaves. They grew from within; they were not added from without. Read John Henry Newman's *Essay on the Development of Christian Doctrine*. Doctrine grew like a plant, not like a crystal: from within, not from without. It's a body, it's organic, it's alive.

PROTESTANT: We clearly contradict each other here.

CATHOLIC: Then let's find out who is right.

PROTESTANT: Sure, but how?

CATHOLIC: First, let's agree about how we disagree. Both of us agree that Catholics believe more things than Protestants do, but we disagree about whether these "more" things are right or wrong, true or false, barnacles on the boat or branches on the tree.

PROTESTANT: You mean things like Church infallibility, the papacy, praying to saints, Purgatory, the Marian dogmas, seven sacraments instead of two, the Mass, transubstantiation, and so forth.

CATHOLIC: Yes.

PROTESTANT: OK, but how can we argue about all these things at once?

CATHOLIC: By judging them all by a single principle: their historical origin—by looking at the history of the Church, to see whether these are barnacles or branches; alien growths from outside or organic growths from within; compromises with paganism or unfoldings of the Gospel. Did the Church always believe these things, from the beginning, at least in embryonic form, or were they new?

PROTESTANT: So you claim that if only you study Church history, you will become a Catholic.

CATHOLIC: Precisely.

PROTESTANT: No, it's not that simple. Your principle of tracing everything back to the beginning is right. But the "beginning" is ultimately not what we find in Church history but what we find in the New Testament. So both sides, in order to adjudicate their differences, must first of all go there, to the only infallible standard they have in common.

CATHOLIC: Fine. In fact, that is exactly what Vatican II and the new *Catechism of the Catholic Church* did. Instead of adding more definitions and creeds and anathemas, the Church turned back to her ultimate sources in scripture. Protestants who read the new catechism are usually very pleasantly surprised at the extent to which the Church claims to base all her teachings on scripture, including the teachings Protestants disagree with the most. Theologians call this return to the sources *ressourcement*. It implies what they call "a hermeneutic of continuity" rather than "a hermeneutic of discontinuity".

PROTESTANT: What does that mean?

CATHOLIC: A "hermeneutic" means an interpretation. The two terms—"a hermeneutic of continuity" and "a hermeneutic of discontinuity"—originated in a conflict about how to interpret the place of the Second Vatican Council in Church history. Both liberal, or left-wing, Catholics and extremely conservative, "traditionalist", right-wing Catholics embraced a hermeneutic of discontinuity because they saw Vatican II as a break with the past, as discontinuous with it, as contradicting it. The far-left liberals said that the Church before Vatican II was wrong and that Vatican II was right, while the far-right conservatives said that the Church before Vatican II was right and that Vatican II was wrong; but both saw Vatican II as something radically new, discontinuous with and contradicting the "pre–Vatican II Church". But every single pope since Vatican II has said that both the left and the right were wrong about this hermeneutic of discontinuity.

PROTESTANT: That has nothing to do with me. I'm not a Catholic.

CATHOLIC: It has a lot to do with you. It's a parallel, an analogy. Catholics have a hermeneutic of continuity not just about Vatican II but also about two thousand years of Church history as a whole, while Protestants have a hermeneutic of discontinuity. You Protestants say the same two things about the Catholic Church as the right-wing conservatives say about Vatican II: that it's a new thing and that it's wrong.

PROTESTANT: OK, that's a kind of map of how we differ about Church history. But it doesn't solve the question of who is right.

CATHOLIC: Yes it does, if the hermeneutic of continuity is right. If it's right, then the history of the Catholic Church goes back through the early Church to Christ, who founded and authorized the Church and her sacraments.

PROTESTANT: It does go back to Christ, but the hermeneutic of continuity is wrong. The medieval Church broke away from her early purity and from Christ. That's the ultimate reason why we are not Catholics: we believe that the Catholic Church contradicts Christ.

CATHOLIC: Did the Apostles contradict Christ?

PROTESTANT: No.

CATHOLIC: Did the early Church—the Church of the Apostles and their immediate disciples—contradict Christ?

PROTESTANT: No.

CATHOLIC: Then the heresy or apostasy began some time later.

PROTESTANT: Yes.

CATHOLIC: That's not what you find if you read Church history. There's no sharp break anywhere.

PROTESTANT: It was gradual, not sharp.

CATHOLIC: But there were no controversies about the issues that divide Protestants and Catholics today. There were controversies, all right, in the early Church, but they were almost always about the Trinity and about the two natures of Christ. Whenever something "Catholic" like Mary or the Real Presence is mentioned, we find only the Catholic view, not the Protestant view. For instance, with the exception of clearly heretical sects like the Cathars or the Albigensians in the Middle Ages, *nobody* doubted or denied the Real Presence of Christ in the Eucharist. Nobody took the usual Protestant position that it's just a holy symbol. And nobody taught *sola scriptura* or "justification by faith alone" rather than justification by faith plus the works of love, until the Reformation.

PROTESTANT: You can't decide such things by the appeal to Church history, which is uncertain; you must decide such things only by the New Testament, which is certain.

CATHOLIC: So you are appealing to *sola scriptura*.

PROTESTANT: Exactly.

CATHOLIC: So you are appealing to *sola scriptura* to prove Protestant principles like *sola scriptura*. Have you ever heard of the logical fallacy of begging the question? That's your fallacy number one. And here's your fallacy number two: you try to get an infallible scripture from a fallible source: the Apostles who wrote it and the Church who defined it. You can't give what you don't have. The effect can't exceed the cause. And here's your fallacy number three about *sola scriptura*. It's a historical fallacy. In historical fact there *was* no New Testament for a generation or so after Christ, but there was a Church from the beginning. The Church is older than the New Testament. It came from her, and she came from Christ. But scripture did not come directly from Christ. Christ wrote nothing. But He did found the Church.

PROTESTANT: You exalt the Church to the same infallible level as Christ.

CATHOLIC: As we both do to scripture—because He created the Church and gave her His authority: "He who hears you hears me" (Lk 10:16). But Christ didn't directly write the New Testament. He wrote nothing, except on the ground (Jn 8:6).

PROTESTANT: Our difference is deeper than just the Church versus scripture—it's the Church versus Christ. You say, "Come to Church." We say, "Come to Christ."

CATHOLIC: So do we. We say, "Come to Church *because the Church is Christ's Body*." If I say "Come to me", I don't mean just "Come to my mind." I mean "Come to where my body is." I am where my body is. Christ was not a philosopher like Buddha who saved us by giving us His mind. He saved us by giving us His Body. He didn't save us by saying, "This is My mind, given to you." He saved us by saying, "This is My Body, given for you."

PROTESTANT: On the Cross, yes.

CATHOLIC: And in the Eucharist. He didn't say those words from the Cross. He said those words at the Last Supper. That's what we invite you to come to: not just the Church but Christ Himself in the Eucharist. You left that. Come home. Come back to Christ. He is really here.

PROTESTANT: And what we say to you is the same thing: Come back to Christ. Like the Church of Ephesus in Revelation 2:4, you have forgotten your first love.

CATHOLIC: And we say that it is you who have forgotten your first love, or at least the Body of your first love, both the Church and the Eucharist; for both are the Body of Christ. You have forgotten your first love, which the early Church had: the whole Christ, Head and Body.

PROTESTANT: That's not true. We have not forgotten Him. We adore Him and His will.

CATHOLIC: Yes, you do. Wonderful. But you have forgotten His will to establish the visible Church as His teaching authority. You have forgotten His real presence not just in your worshipping souls but in the Eucharist itself. And that is inexcusable, because it is in scripture as well as Church teaching.

PROTESTANT: And we say that it is you who have forgotten Christ, for your building has obscured its foundation, your so-called fuller Christ has obscured Christ Himself, like the moon eclipsing the sun. The moon of your Church has stood between you and the sun of God. Your fireplace has put out its own fire; and a fireplace without a fire is even more worthless than a fire without a fireplace. Christianity is essentially a fire, the fire Christ came to light (Lk 3:16; 12:49). We do not see that fire in you.

CATHOLIC: Really? You don't see the fire of Christ in the eyes of John Paul II and Mother Teresa?

PROTESTANT: We don't see it in the average Joe Six-Pack Catholic.

CATHOLIC: Perhaps you should look more carefully. Watch him as he worships on Sunday morning. Watch him stop breathing at the moment of consecration. Do Protestants have such a holy moment, such a worshipful posture of body and soul every Sunday morning?

PROTESTANT: Only God can judge hearts. We're getting too judgmental.

CATHOLIC: You're right. We should argue about objective truth, not subjective piety. So let's look at the objective historical facts. It's really very simple. It all comes down to the fact that Christ established a visible Church. If you accept Christ, and His will, you must accept His Church. We didn't invent it; He did. You want to meet him? Good. But the Church is the means He founded for you to meet Him and for Him to meet you, to meet across the centuries. Her sacraments are like hoses that get the living water to you across the distance of time. These Catholic things that you reject as superstitions and heresies are precisely the God-ordained matches to light that fire that you love.

PROTESTANT: You have it backward. You can't get Christ out of the Church, like getting orange juice out of an orange. You said we get the Church from Christ, because He gave her to us, and that's right (even though we think you're wrong about her being infallible). But now you're saying the opposite: that you get Christ from the Church. You don't. You don't get Christ out of the Church and her sacraments as you get orange juice out of an orange. The Church doesn't squeeze Christ-juice out of herself and feed you; the Church points to Christ, brings you to Christ, by witnessing to you of Christ, like a missionary, a saint, an evangelist, a prophet.

CATHOLIC: She does that too, of course, but she's more than that. You're reducing the Body of Christ to a prophet, but it's also a priest, like Christ Himself. A prophet is a mouth, a voice from God. But the Church is more than His voice; she is His Body. That's why you can indeed get Christ from the Church today, as you get orange juice from an orange, because He put Himself into her, as the Creator put orange juice into oranges.

PROTESTANT: That's superstition and idolatry and material-ism and paganism. That's not the Gospel. We left the Cath-olic Church—Luther left—because Christ's Gospel was no longer being preached. Catholics didn't know how to get saved. They thought it was by receiving the sacraments, like magic, and doing enough good works—a kind of legal magic. They were heretics: materialists, externalists, superstitious.

CATHOLIC: Both sides were morally at fault in the Reformation, and maybe Catholic motives were even more morally faulty than Protestant ones—no one but God can read hearts. But it is you who were the theological heretics: you were and are Gnostics, spiritualists.

PROTESTANT: What do you mean by that?

CATHOLIC: We don't first get saved in a purely spiritual and invisible and individual way, in the soul, and only then, after that, come together into the Church, the visible community. We get saved precisely by entering the community, by baptism, as Noah's family got saved from the Flood by entering the ark. (By the way, did you know that the New Testament clearly says that "baptism . . . saves you"? Read 1 Peter 3:21.) The Church is the ark of salvation. God provided her for us, that we would enter her and be saved. Like Christ, it's both visible and invisible. You're Gnostics because you deny the visible, the material dimension, of Christ.

PROTESTANT: We don't deny it; we just don't make it infallible. And we're not spiritualists—you are materialists. It is you who lack the fullness of Christ because you neglect the personal, the invisible, which is even more central.

CATHOLIC: No, we have both.

PROTESTANT: If you have both, why isn't the average Catholic as saintly as the average Evangelical Protestant?

CATHOLIC: We have far more saints than you do.

PROTESTANT: No, you don't—you just canonize more of them. And even if you do have more, it is only more of the public, famous, spectacular ones. And you certainly also have more sinners, and more spectacular sinners.

CATHOLIC: Well, that's true. And that's to be expected. Hospitals have the sickest people in them. The Church is a hospital for sinners, not a museum for saints.

~

It is time to stop and reflect on this typical acrimonious debate. Has it degenerated into judgmental name calling? Or has it finally emerged into a productive competition between saint makers? Wouldn't that be a good way to keep score?—whoever produces the most saints will win the game and win the world. Maybe that is such a good competition that God keeps the two churches apart from each other just to elicit that competition. And maybe, at some future time, the game will be over, both sides will win, and the two teams will declare a draw and a mutual victory because the world will be won for Christ by a thousand Mother Teresas. (I suspect it would take only about ten.)

~

When we first look at the argument, the two sides seem hopelessly at odds. Then we begin to notice how both appeal to the same thing: Christ. The Christocentric motive of both sides is the same.

And the method of arguing, the standard appealed to, is also the same: beginnings, foundations. If a Protestant and a

Catholic could only take a time machine back to A.D. 29 and ask Christ Himself which kind of church is His will, both would willingly and eagerly convert to the other's church if Christ Himself willed it. So, lacking that time machine, they both do the next best thing: turn to historical memory, aided by documents, beginning with the New Testament.

And that is the secret of the ecumenical progress that has been made in the last 50 years (e.g., the Decree on Justification; see chapter 2), which is far greater progress than has been made in the previous 450. We are more than halfway home. We have many (a) theological and (b) institutional obstacles to overcome, but (c) our motives, which are the very first thing, have been massively converted: (c1) we love each other, and (c2) we love each other's faith in Christ, and (c3) we want to learn from each other, because (c4) we both have a holy greed for all that we can learn of Christ, for all that Christ has to teach us through each other, for all the glues that can glue us to Christ more tightly, no matter how different they are, if they only really glue us tighter to Him; and (c5) we are both distressed at the wounds and lacerations in His Body, as Paul was (1 Cor 1–2) and as Christ Himself was (Jn 17).

Christ will use these motives, these demands, these loves. He is doing it already. He will not ignore them. It is impossible that they will not bear fruit. It is also impossible that we can at present see what form that fruit will take.

9

What Is the Eucharist?

If Protestants are right, then Catholics are making a really ridiculous mistake. Catholics are bowing to bread and worshipping wine, thinking it is literally Jesus Christ. That is not only idolatry—that is insanity.

If Catholics are right, then Protestants are missing out on the most real, total, perfect union with Christ that is possible in this life, a gift He Himself left to us as His most precious gift of all: Himself, in person, really and fully and truly and completely present, Body and Blood, soul and divinity, hiding beneath the appearances of the Eucharistic bread and wine, playing peek-a-boo with us as a loving father does with his little baby.

The issue of Christ's Real Presence in the Eucharist is not merely a simple either-or, it is complex. But it is still an either-or. He is either really there, or not.

Yes, it is complex. The Protestant Reformers argued among themselves about the Eucharist and developed more than one alternative to the Catholic position. Anglo-Catholics are quite close to the Catholic understanding; Lutherans a little less so, Presbyterians and Methodists much less so, Baptists even farther away (for them it is only a symbol, like a picture or a word). Some say Jesus is present only in the soul of the person who receives the Eucharist; or in the Church's act of celebrating it or the individual's act of receiving it; or as He is present in other sincere and holy exchanges such as prayer, or reading or hearing the Bible in faith. No, says the Church: He is just as truly and fully in the Eucharist as He was in Mary's house or on the Cross.

There is a great difference even between the Catholic teaching of "transubstantiation" and the Lutheran teaching of "consubstantiation"—that Christ is really present "along with" the bread and wine, which remain bread and wine. The Catholic Church insists that that is not bread and wine anymore, after the consecration. It looks like bread and wine, but that is literally Jesus Christ in disguise. There was a substantial change, an essential change, from bread and wine to Christ. The change from an acorn to an oak is not a substantial change, but the change from a live oak to dead, rotting wood is a substantial change. Three examples of substantial change in our lives are (a) conception, (b) death, and (c) resurrection. The change that happens at the consecration in the Mass is as great as the change that will happen to us as it happened to Christ at His Resurrection.

The fundamental dispute about the Eucharist is not just about truth but about being, not just about theology but about reality, not just about who is theologically *right* here, but about Who *is* here. Is that thing that we swallow Christ, or is it just holy bread? Should we worship and adore that thing that looks like a little piece of bread, or not? Whichever answer to that question is wrong is very wrong indeed.

Suppose you are in doubt not just about who is *right* here

in their Eucharistic theology but about who is right-*here*, in the church under the little red altar light. How can you move from doubting to knowing?

If you are in doubt and really want to know, I suggest a way to find out, whether you are Protestant, Catholic, or neither. You could read good books about it, of course, from both sides; and there is nothing wrong with that. But I suggest a simpler and more radical method.

Go into a Catholic church, where the Eucharist is reserved in the Tabernacle on the altar, and the little red lamp near it is lit to signify that the consecrated Host is there. If you honestly and sincerely and passionately want to know whether that is profound truth or profound error, then pray something like this prayer and mean it:

"God, You know everything that is in my mind and heart. You know that I want to know the truth, and live according to it, *whatever* it is. And if my motive is not really as pure and honest and open-minded as that, then You also know that I *want* to be totally honest and open, which is why I am asking You to purify my motives, so that I am totally open to the truth, whatever it is.

"You know that I'm in doubt about this thing, this thing that divides the two branches of Western Christendom. Is that really You there, God the Son, eternal and divine and to be adored and worshipped as my Lord and trusted with my eternal soul as my Savior? Or is that only a holy symbol of You, so that this Catholic doctrine and this part of Catholic worship is a big mistake, however sincerely motivated those people may be, and however pleasing to You these Catholics may be in other ways? *Is that really You there, or not?*

"Please let me know, in Your own time and Your own way. I can't hold you to a timetable, but I do believe Your Word, so I hold You to Your promise: "Seek and you shall find." I will believe and confess and live whatever truth You lead me to.

"I want only Your truth, whatever it is. And if You see that I'm not really as honest and single-minded as that, then You also see that I want to be as honest and single-minded as that. If truth is not the only thing I want, it's the only thing I want to want. If I can't say I want only that 'Thy will, not mine, be done', I can at least say that I want to want that. God, be merciful to me, for my soul is full of sins and divisions as well as ignorance. The only thing I can wholly trust is Your mercy.

"You know every secret of my heart. Here, now, in prayer, heart-to-heart with You, face-to-face with You at this moment, I put my seal on what I just said: I say 'Amen' to that."

What will happen next? If you really want to know, ask God, not me.

I mean it. Do it—don't just think about it. Can it do any harm? Can loving and seeking the truth do any harm? Can Christ do any harm? Can total honesty before God do any harm? Is there anything to fear from infinite divine love? No. Therefore, just say, "Jesus, I trust You." Those words please Him immensely.

10

My First Original Evangelical Thought and My First Original Catholic Thought

I don't remember how old I was when I had my first original Evangelical thought. I think I was somewhere between five and ten. But though I don't remember the time, I remember the place vividly. It was in the family car driving home (west) on Haledon Avenue, just passing the corner of North Eighth Street, on a Sunday morning after church and Sunday school. I had been somewhat confused by all the many things I had heard Sunday after Sunday from the preacher, Rev. Ted Jansma, who was a very good one: bad preachers don't ever wake up their congregation enough to confuse them. I turned to my father, who was an elder in the Sixth Reformed Church of Paterson, New Jersey, a man of great practical wisdom, honesty, and common sense; and I said, "Dad, all that different stuff we learn in church and Sunday school—it all comes down to just one thing, doesn't it?"

I was sitting in the front seat. My mother was sitting in the back seat. I remember that because it was usually the opposite. (My father was not a male chauvinist.) I don't know why I got to sit next to my father that day. He looked over at me with surprise and, I imagine, some suspicion. "What do you mean, only one thing? The Bible teaches us many things, and they're all important."

"Yeah, but it's all about one thing, isn't it?"

"Just one thing? What do you think that is?" I clearly remember his tone of voice. It sounded like a schoolteacher's benign patience with the oversimplifications of a little kid.

"Well, we just have to ask Jesus what He wants us to do, and then do it. All the time."

He looked over at me with a smile that showed surprise and respect. "You're absolutely right, son, you're absolutely right."

Of course, it was divine inspiration, not inherent natural wisdom. But I felt proud of it anyway, and still do ("Unless you turn and become like children . . ." [Mt 18:3])— because adults typically lose the simple when they learn the complex, miss the forest for the trees. Everything in Christianity is a tree in that forest, as every word in the Bible is an atom in His face.

~

I think it was a few years later, but still in my preteen years, when I had my first Catholic thought. My parents and I often went to New York City as tourists. We lived only eighteen miles west of the George Washington Bridge. One Saturday we went to Saint Patrick's Cathedral. I had never been in a cathedral before. All the churches I knew were simple Protestant and rather Puritan-style churches. Entering this space—a new *kind* of space—I was stunned to silence. I stopped walking. I even stopped breathing for a minute. This was something different not just in degree but in kind from anything I had ever seen before. It was not only beautiful—it was holy.

I turned to my father. "Dad, this is a Catholic church, isn't it?"

"Yes, it is."

"The Catholics are wrong, aren't they?"

"Oh, yes. Very wrong."

"Then how come their churches are so beautiful?"

For the first time in my life, I saw my father stumped. I don't remember what his answer was, but it wasn't good enough to remember. The cathedral, on the other hand, was unforgettable.

Is that any kind of reason or argument? Yes, it is, though it is not a proof of anything. It is eloquent. It says something. Words are not the only kind of speech. There are "sermons in stone".

I know three ex-agnostics (two philosophers and one monk) who told me that when they had real doubts and were dabbling with atheism, the thing that convinced them most strongly that God was real was listening to Bach's *Saint Matthew Passion*. They all said something like this: "That music makes sense only if God is real. In a world without God, that music isn't real. But it *is* real. Therefore, there must be a God." You just see that. Or you don't.

Later, I read Saint John of the Cross, out of idle curiosity. I had read some good Protestant saints, but never anything like this. They were good, green little hills; this was a fjord, an Everest. I didn't understand it, but I knew it was somehow massively true. You just know that. You just see it. Or you don't.

~

There were my first original Protestant thought and my first original Catholic thought. They do not oppose or exclude each other, and the Church is missing something necessary and essential if she does not understand and teach both of them.

11

Who Has the "Full Gospel"?

We all want it. But what is it? And who has it?

Is it a quantitative thing, so that the more you believe, the better, unless it is heresy? But what is heresy and what isn't?

I have called it the "math of more" (see p. 30, above). But this quantitative standard not only fails to give us an automatic answer but also raises crucial questions about quantity.

Let's look first at the obvious surface difference: it is indeed a difference in quantity. Protestants fault Catholics for believing too many things, things in the Bible *plus*. Catholics fault Protestants for believing too little: only that part of Sacred Tradition that they find explicitly in the Bible. Let's see what happens to this quantity when someone has a religious conversion.

When a humanist becomes a theist, he comes to believe more, not less. As a humanist, he believed in man, but now he also believes in God. And what happens to the things he already believes? He loses nothing in humanism but strengthens and perfects it. If man is made in the image of God, if man is God's beloved child, then man is more, not less

60

—more valuable, more wonderful, more called to heroic heights—than if he is only the child of man.

Another example: When a Jew becomes a Christian, he comes to believe more, but not less. He loses nothing in Judaism but fulfills it. He is now a completed Jew. Jews who become Christians almost always say that. Jesus Himself said that He came not to destroy (or reduce) "the law and the prophets" (i.e., Jewish tradition; Mt 5:17) but to bring them to fulfillment, just as humanists who become theists add to their humanism and also increase it and fulfill it.

Analogously, when a Protestant becomes a Catholic, he loses nothing positive in Protestantism but perfects it.

Most Protestant converts say that. I do. I am far more appreciative of Evangelicalism, of the Bible, of Christocentrism, and of the absolute dependence on divine grace now as a Catholic than I ever was as a Protestant.

But what happens when the conversion works the other way? What happens when Catholics convert to Protestantism?

Let's look at positive cases, not negative ones—I mean cases where the converts say they have added rather than subtracted and discarded. Not cases where they said there was just too much in the Catholic Church to believe and they left in disgust or disbelief but cases where they say they found something positive in a Protestant church that they didn't find in their Catholic church.

These converts also say that they now believe more than they did before, not less, even though as Protestants they believe fewer dogmas. Why? Listen to what they say. They found *Christ*. Nothing could be more positive than that.

I'm talking about deeply religious conversions now rather

than something silly and shallow like a preference for "Christian rock music" over Gregorian chant, or finding a certain local Protestant congregation friendlier to them than the local Catholic one. Those are bad examples for two reasons. First, good luck in finding a Catholic congregation that does Gregorian chant. Second, Christian rock is not only theologically shallow (to prove that to yourself, just say the lyrics aloud to yourself without the music) but also musically shallow: an embarrassment and an insult to rock as well as to Christianity.

So the converts in opposite directions (from Catholic to Protestant and from Protestant to Catholic) do not differ on the principle that everything positive is to be embraced and everything negative is to be rejected. They differ on what is positive. For instance, Protestants would maintain that Luther's three *solas* are positive, not negative, as Catholics see them.

Those are experiential data. Now, how do we explain those data? How do we map these murky waters?

Here is one principle to start with. We should not define truth by quantity. "I believe more than you do; therefore, I'm right." Use of that standard would not only rank Catholicism over Protestantism but also Mormonism or Swedenborgianism over Catholicism, and polytheism over monotheism.

Another principle: Protestants should not *define* themselves negatively, as protesters against Catholicism. If they did that, then they would be dependent on Catholicism, so that if all Catholics died or apostatized or left this planet, Protestants could no longer exist because they would have nothing to define themselves over against. Once that against which you protest ceases to be anything, your protest ceases to mean anything. There are no abolitionists in America anymore because there is no slavery anymore.

The point is that your denials of the other's beliefs should not be the condition for defining your own belief. Catholics and Protestants should not define themselves by each other. That cannot be their essence. Therefore, it should not be essential for Protestants to deny Catholic beliefs in order to be Protestants, and it should not be essential for Catholics to deny Protestant beliefs in order to be Catholics.

Unless, of course, the two beliefs logically contradict each other, so that the denial of the other positive belief logically follows from the affirmation of your own positive belief. For instance, to believe the essential positive Christian claim about Jesus, that He is not only the perfect man, the greatest man who ever lived, but also the Son of God, is necessarily to deny the Muslim's positive belief that Muhammad, not Jesus, is the greatest man who ever lived. And to say that the Bible is infallible necessarily entails the rejection of the Muslim belief that the Qur'an is infallible, because the Qur'an clearly denies that Jesus is the Son of God and that the Christian Bible is infallible. The Bible doesn't mention the Qur'an, but the Qur'an mentions the Bible.

But these two beliefs, Protestantism and Catholicism, certainly *seem* to contradict each other. Yes, they seem to, but your faith should not depend on anything that is only a "seems to", on what seems to contradict what, on a "perhaps". And that *is* a "perhaps": perhaps these two really do contradict, but perhaps they don't, and perhaps we can come to see that. That is what happened regarding the single most important issue of the Reformation, justification by faith. (See chapter 2.) We don't know for sure that resolution can't happen with regard to other apparent contradictions. And what we don't know for sure should not define our faith. As Catholics we do know for sure that all the dogmas defined and taught by the Church Christ founded and authorized to teach in His name are true; we do not know for sure which of those dogmas really, and not just apparently, contradict which teachings in other religions. The Church rarely tells us that. She defines and defends her dogmas in response to heretics who deny them, but she does not directly meddle in the affairs of other religions, unless they explicitly reject hers. "If anyone denies this, let him be anathema" is her formula. Notice the "iffyness". E.g., she (1) reveals the positive fact that Mary was immaculately conceived without sin, and (2) says that "*if* anyone denies this, he is in error", but she does not tell us concretely who is making that error.

A concrete example: Saint Thomas Aquinas, the single most authoritative and relied-on Catholic theologian in history, denied the Immaculate Conception, because he misunderstood it. Like Protestants today, he rightly said that every human being descended from Adam and Eve needs salvation from Original Sin. And since Mary was descended from Adam and Eve, she too needed salvation from Original Sin. Therefore, she could not have been totally sinless, free from Original Sin as well as all actual, personal sins. Saint Thomas said this centuries before the dogma was defined by the Church. He was wrong about Mary's Immaculate Conception but right about his general principle that all humans need salvation. Mary was saved from committing actual sins by being saved from Original Sin, but she was saved by Christ. Like us, she had to be saved from both Original Sin and actual sins, but she was saved from actual sins in a different way than we are. She was saved from falling (in the future), while we are saved from having fallen (in the past); she was saved before she fell (or would have fallen), while we are saved after we fell. God saved her by blocking Original Sin from entering her at her conception; He saves us by removing Original Sin, by baptism, after we contracted that disease. She got preventive medicine; we got healing medicine. Same God, same grace, same need for salvation by supernatural intervention, but different methods. God's ways are manifold and unpredictable and incredibly imaginative.

The relevance of this issue about Mary to the ecumenical issue is that even when two sides seem to contradict each other because one side believes something the other does not (as Duns Scotus believed in the Immaculate Conception and Thomas Aquinas did not), sometimes there is no real contradiction. We can't be wrong about what God reveals, but we can be wrong about our own interpretations of it. So we should claim certainty only about the positive things God has revealed ("God said it, I believe it, that settles it"), but we should not claim certainty, only probability, about whether the positive things we believe really, and not just apparently, contradict and negate the positive things other religions or other churches believe. And this principle should apply not only to ecumenical dialogue between Protestants and Catholics but also to interfaith dialogue between Christians and believers in other world religions: the definition of one faith should not *depend on* the negation of another.

That does not mean there are not many real contradictions (there are) or that "deep down we're all saying the same thing in different words" (we're not). It means that even when we rightly say, "God said it, I believe it, that settles it", we can't know that when we claim that "it" is true and someone else claims that "it" is not true the two of us are talking about exactly the same "it". Our certainty is vertical, not horizontal.

Of course, there are real contradictions between religions, e.g., between polytheism and monotheism. Many of the apparent contradictions are real. To deny this and to claim that all religious disputes are only misunderstandings feels good, but that total "inclusivism" can't stand up to careful, honest, open-minded investigation of the issues. But I am saying that we can't be sure that all of these apparent contradictions are real contradictions (let's call that "total exclusivism") and that we can't be sure which ones are real and which ones are only apparent.

The only other religion the Bible explicitly rejects in toto is idolatry, polytheism. It says nothing about "comparative religions" in general, and nothing about religions it does not know about, e.g., Hinduism, Buddhism, Taoism, Confucianism, and Islam. (However, Islam says something explicit about Christianity: that its central dogma, that Christ is the Son of God, is false.)

Jesus was a Jew. Jews labeled Samaritans as heretics. But when Jesus conversed with the heretical Samaritan woman (Jn 4), He said nothing negative about her heretical beliefs. Nor did He affirm them. But He did address them. He negotiated the divisive "worship in Samaria versus worship in Jerusalem" issue, which seemed to be a clear contradiction, by transcending it. That seemed impossible, for the two positions logically contradicted each other. Is Jerusalem God's one divinely appointed Temple where all should worship and where alone worship was authentic and divinely instituted, or not? Were Samaritans, who worshipped elsewhere, right or wrong?

In some ways, at least, this was very similar to the Protestant-Catholic issue: Is the Catholic Church the one true Church, or is God pleased with Protestant churches too? Is He really present in the Eucharist only when it is consecrated by Catholic priests who have holy orders by apostolic succession, or not? Are Anglican orders invalid, as the Catholic Church claims, or are they valid, as Anglicans claim?

The law of noncontradiction seems to make it impossible to transcend this issue. One must either ignore it, or say one side is right and therefore the other one is wrong—unless one is a muddleheaded irrationalist like Walt Whitman, who wrote, "Do I contradict myself? Very well, then, I contradict myself. I am large. I contain multitudes."[1]

God is not "large" by being muddleheaded. But He is "large" in other ways, ways that transcend human possibilities of "largeness". One of the marks of God's presence is doing what to us seems impossible. "With God all things are possible" (Mt 19:26).

In other words, we do not understand much at all. We are all shallow, shortsighted, and stupid. That is God's answer to Job. That is the divine revelation we most often love to forget. But it is reasonable to believe that. If even on a human level "there are more things in heaven and earth than are dreamt of in your philosophy", as Hamlet said to Horatio, then how much more must there be more things in God than are dreamed of in all our philosophies? If only we began with a vivid remembering of that Socratic principle of "learned ignorance", and did not conveniently forget it as we proceeded, we might make "impossible" progress in ecumenism.

---

[1] "Song of Myself".

Both in ecumenical (Protestant-Catholic) dialogue and in interfaith dialogue between different world religions, each side (1) first affirms its distinctive doctrine because it expresses what that group sees as something positive, an affirmation, an insight; and (2) then, derivatively, in light of that, judges other religions wrong because they seem to lack it. Which of these two kinds of understanding, (1) or (2), is more likely to be true and accurate and adequate: your positive understanding of your own belief or your negative understanding of the other's?

The personal can't help intruding on the objective when it comes to religion. Religion is not about "problems" but about "mysteries", to use Marcel's famous distinction—it is about truths we are passionately involved in personally, not about things we can abstract ourselves from, like mathematics. There have been mutual polemics, over many centuries, that were motivated by strong, even nonnegotiably strong, personal passions. How could this not have narrowed our vision? How could it not have dug ruts and stereotypes in the minds of both sides?

You seldom see your enemy's mind clearly. Moving from seeing the other as your enemy to seeing him as your friend is a necessary preliminary to understanding the beliefs of the other. It is not in itself sufficient, but it is necessary.

Every religion demands a strong personal commitment of faith (personal trust and fidelity) and hope (our heart's demand for happiness and joy) and love (which has to be "fanatical", for you have to love God with *your whole heart and mind and soul and strength* [see Deut 6:5]). Compromise is forbidden. Tepidity is forbidden. If we are lukewarm, our God will vomit us out of His mouth. (That is exactly what He said! Look it up: Rev 3:16.) Religious dialogue among the lukewarm always ends in platitudes. Only religious dialogue among the hot, not among the lukewarm, can melt the walls between us.

But how? Our first teacher in ecumenism should be Christ, and our second one should be Socrates, who was wise because he knew he lacked wisdom. Both teach us humility. Socrates says we must be either fools because we think we are wise, or wise because we know we are fools. Christ says we must be either sinners who think we are saints, or saints who know we are sinners. Even outside religion, and much more inside, there are many things we can come to understand only after we come to know that we don't understand. In fact, most of the really important things in life are like that.

If that is Lesson One, what is Lesson Two? I think Lesson Two is to keep going back to Lesson One, because we are fatally prone to forget Lesson One once we look at Lesson Two.

12

Passion

Even the great rationalist and "absentminded professor" Hegel knew that in human history "nothing great has ever been accomplished without passion."[1] Since reuniting the Church is something great, it is one of those things that cannot be accomplished without passion. Passion alone is not sufficient, but it is necessary. It is not just going to happen. Did you ever see a bumper sticker that says "Reunion Happens"?

The right object of infinite passion is only something infinite. Reunion itself as a "cause" to rally around is not something infinite. But Truth is. Reunion must be for the sake of truth, and only in truth, never in compromise of truth.

And for the Christian, truth is not primarily an abstract relationship between an idea and a fact; truth is a divine Person. Jesus Christ is the Truth, the Mind of God. He is not just true—He is Truth. At the Transfiguration, light shone not on Him but from Him. We dare not instrumentalize Him, use Him as a means to further ends, even good ends. We may not do that even to human persons. Persons

[1] Georg Wilhelm Friedrich Hegel, *The Philosophy of History.*

are ends, absolutes. That is what love recognizes: love treats other persons as ends, as absolute goods. If we dare not instrumentalize each other, we certainly dare not instrumentalize the God-man.

So how does that apply to ecumenism and reunion? It means we must not come to Him for the sake of reunion, but we must come to Him as the One for the sake of whom reunion must happen. He is the end, not a means. To put this abstract point more concretely and personally, we must be *with* Him when He prays "that they may all be one" (Jn 17:21). We must look not only *at* Him but also *with* Him. We must look with His eyes. We must judge ourselves by His mind and not judge Him by our mind. That is not just a clever thing to say—that is a necessary thing actually to do. To see how hard that is to do, try to do it right now. Try to judge what is in your mind now, your reaction to that very point that you are thinking about, the idea that you just read, by letting His mind judge yours rather than vice versa. Don't try to figure out His mind—that is a kind of "judging" of His mind; just passionately open your mind to His, like a woman in love opening her body and her life to her husband. Thinking should be like lovemaking. That is why its product is called a "conception". It is a product of passion.

The very best kind of thinking is praying.

In our ecumenical dialogues we must never forget, for one moment, that He, and nothing less, is our absolute. We all have Attention Deficit Disorder; we all forget the most important things a thousand times a day. So the best we can do is constant, repeated repentance and conversion, turning around, turning back to Him every time we remember that we have forgotten Him. That is not just private piety;

that must motivate our dialoguing. Religious dialogue is a form of the constant conversion to Christ that all the recent popes and all the recent apparitions of Mary have called for.

We cannot reunite unless we understand each other better. We cannot understand each other better unless we listen to each other better. We cannot listen to each other better unless we listen to Christ better. Listening to each other is not enough: the right motive, the Christocentric motive, for listening to each other is equally necessary.

The thing itself—mutual listening—is much harder to do than we think, though it is a necessity in all kinds of human negotiations: in families, in Congress, in friendships, in religion. Most of the time when we think we are listening, we are just waiting for the opportunity to answer. Good listeners are much, much rarer than good talkers.

Saints make the best ecumenists. What would happen on the ecumenical front if all two billion Christians in the world were as saintly as Mother Teresa? The essential answer is very clear and predictable, though the details would be surprising and unpredictable. If all Christians were saints, we would understand each other and the Church would be one —one rich tapestry of nondivisive diversities. We would live the formula "In essentials, unity; in nonessentials, diversity; in all things, charity." And we would much more clearly understand what those "essentials" are, what is and what is not essential. We differ about that now, we differ about the first two parts of that three-part formula, ultimately because we do not sufficiently live the third and most important part. We do not live in passionate charity; we are not yet saints.

So let's get on with it. Our Lord is waiting.

13

Three Reasons for Reunion

What are the compelling reasons for reunion? There are three.

First and foremost, our Lord demands it. It is not an "ideal"—it is a command.

Second, the Church demands it. Saint Paul demands it (1 Cor 1). Both "sides" of the divide demand it. Catholics demand it, and Biblical Protestants demand it. The Reformation's original goal was not to create another church forever but to reform and purify the old one. And the Catholic Church is equally adamant about unity: read John Paul II's *Ut Unum Sint*.

Third, the world needs it. Western civilization (which used to be "Christendom") is dying. Its humanistic education, its literacy, its historical memory, its identity, its spirit, its reason for being, its hope, its ultimate end, the very idea that there is such a thing as an "ultimate end", are all dying. All civilizations die, but some live longer than others, and some recover from life-threatening diseases. The dictatorship of relativism and the justification of moral decadence is a life-threatening disease. Christophobia is a deadly disease, and it has infected many, perhaps even most, of our culture's mind molders, the intellectuals, the teachers, both formal (in the schools) and informal (in the media).

But this tremendous crisis can be a tremendous opportunity. We stare at a civilization-sized, Christ-shaped vacuum. If we obey Christ's "great commission" (Mt 18:28) to preach the good news, if we show them Christ, we will save not only souls but also society. When we apply the golden key to the lock, we fill the hole, we bind up the lacerations. We heal.

The opposite of healing is dying. Civilizations rarely die suddenly; they go into long, gradual decline, like Alzheimer's patients. Decline eventually becomes death. Religious warfare was the primary cause of the decline of religion in our civilization. It was not the so-called war between Science and Religion. That is a wholly mythical war, a war without a single casualty, without a single religious doctrine refuted by a single scientific discovery. Rather, it is the war between Religion and Religion, i.e., the war between Protestants and Catholics, and, to a lesser extent, the war between Christians and Jews, especially in the past, and, finally, the war between Muslims and Christians in the present and the future. Those wars were and are the primary cause of the skepticism about religion and the rise of pure secularism, and thus of the death of Western civilization; therefore, their opposite, religious love, will be the primary cause of its recovery.

There is no alternative. For a Christ-shaped hole is also a Christ-sized hole, and nothing is big enough to fill a Christ-sized hole except Christ.

And a divided Christendom can hardly heal a divided civilization, because a divided Christendom looks like a divided

Christ. A Christendom divided in itself can hardly claim to reconcile the divided tatters of a civilization. The infected patient can rightly say to the infected doctor, "Physician, heal thyself." A schizophrenic psychiatrist is not the cure for a schizophrenic patient.

14

The Goal of the Reformation

What was the primary goal, end, purpose, and hope of the Protestant Reformation?

To reform the Church, of course. But why? Is that the final end, or is that a means to a still-further end, a response to a more absolute good?

It is the latter, indeed; therefore, the reforms must be judged according to that latter good, that end. What is that greater good? Why reform the Church?

To obey the will of Christ. To restore the fullness of Christ to the Church and to the lives of her members. To make the Church a Veronica's veil, on which the true face of Christ is indelibly imprinted for the world to see. That is the sacred task that pious and holy Protestants seek above all.

It is also the sacred task that pious and holy Catholics seek above all.

Disputes about Church authority and about doctrine must all be judged in that light. When that light shines in the places where these disputes are discussed, all true colors appear. When any other light shines, the colors are skewed. For that light alone, the light of Christ's will, is pure and brings out all true colors. All other lights project their own coloration and somehow distort.

Therefore, the first and most effective means to understand and adjudicate our disputes is not to get the colors right but to get the light right. It is not to get clarity about the disputes themselves, however necessary that is, but to get the clear light of Christ, to let it illuminate all the darkest corners of our souls and our history, to love it with 100 percent of our hearts and minds, and to love nothing else outside of it. The fundamental reason reunion has not happened is that we have not done that: we have not obeyed Saint Paul's command to "have this mind among yourselves, which was in Christ Jesus" (Phil 2:5). Christ-mindedness is our first necessity. This alone will "work".

And this *will* work. I can prove that this will work. I can prove that this single first step—to purify our own minds and motives, a thing that is within our choice—is the infallibly guaranteed road that will in fact lead to reunion if we only take it. Here is my proof. It is ridiculously simple and obvious:

1. Christ's will is unity. That is clear from scripture.

2. Therefore, our disunities are all caused not by His will but by our own. All the cacophony in the Christian orchestra is caused by our looking at our own scripts, our own scores, our own agendas, rather than looking at His. They are caused by substituting our own fingers for the baton of the Conductor of the orchestra.

3. Therefore, if, and insofar as, we look at His baton, His mind, His will, we will play in harmony. It will not be in unison, but it will not be division either. Harmony. He wants harmony.

4. It is first of all a question of a purified will, and then, as a result, a purified mind. We know His mind only insofar as we will His will. (See Jn 7:17.)

5. Therefore, insofar as we will His will more purely and passionately and with more of our hearts and wills, we will achieve that end and reunite His Body.

I do not know when or how, in the short run, these disputes will be solved. I do not have the theological keys to unravel these disputed issues. But I do know how, in the long run, these disputes will be solved: by fixing our whole attention and love on our common Conductor's baton. That principle is embarrassingly simple to understand and embarrassingly hard to do. Let the Conductor of the Christian orchestra conduct.

"Letting Him do it" may sound passive, but it is not; it is extremely active. It is what Mary said: "Let it be to me according to your word" (Lk 1:38). That was not Stoic resignation; that was fanatical and passionate (though quiet) love.

"Unless the Lord builds the house, those who build it labor in vain" (Ps 127:1). Surely that applies most of all to His own house, and to repairing it as well as building it. Because Saint Francis, like Mary, said yes to His Annunciation to him, when He said, "My Church is in ruins; repair it"; because Francis and other saints (Bernard, Bonaventure, Thomas Aquinas) who heard that call rose up like an obedient wind and blew through the world, a great storm of sanctity and wisdom erupted and one of the greatest eras of Christendom happened.

It was meant to continue.

15

Stereotypes and Caricatures

Here are some of the false ideas and stereotypes that many Protestants have about Catholics. I had them myself when I was a kid.

Catholics are idolaters. They worship Mary, and the pope, and the Church, and the saints, and statues, and sacraments.

Catholics are primitive, uneducated, superstitious, animal-like, passionate, emotional, oversexed, overbreeding, medieval, feudal peasants from backward "communitarian" cultures mainly in southern Europe. Protestants are educated, scientific, rational, spiritual, prudent, responsible, self-controlled capitalist entrepreneurs mainly from northern Europe. Catholics are Epicureans; Protestants are Stoics. Stoics are more moral.

Catholics don't believe in freedom or democracy. They believe in authority and hierarchy.

Catholics don't know how to get to Heaven. They think they can buy their way in with a merit pile of good works.

Catholics believe in magic. The sacraments are salvation machines.

Catholics are slaves to history, blind traditionalists.

Now here are some of the false, stereotyped ideas many Catholics have about Protestants.

Protestants are heretics, rebels, autonomous do-it-your-selfers. They rejected God's Church and invented a new one.

Protestants are individualists. "Me and God—that's it."

Protestants are Puritans, Gnostics, spiritualists. They don't really believe in the Incarnation—that is why they're skeptical of the visible Church and sacraments.

Protestants think you don't have to do good works to get to Heaven—you just have to have faith, or be "born again", which to them is a one-time emotional experience. That's it, that's all.

Protestants are slaves to the present. They grant no authority to tradition, history, or the past. They don't know it and don't want to. Soon they'll all become modernists.

It is helpful and clarifying to state these attitudes baldly because the answer to all these problems is the same: not a single sentence above is true. They are all misunderstandings, straw men, exaggerations, caricatures. We have to scrap them all, deny them all, and start over again. How do we start? By listening to each other.

What will happen then? Good things. Surprises. Unpredictable things. Things we can't say because we can't presently see them. Things like the Decree on Justification (see chapter 2).

16

The Plant Metaphor
Applied to Ecumenism

I like to think of faith, hope, and charity, the three greatest things in the world, the three "theological virtues", as three parts of a plant: the root (faith), the stem (hope), and the fruit (love). Faith, hope, and charity are not three things but three stages or aspects of the same thing—not three plants but three components of the one plant.

What plant? The plant is our "divinization" (*theosis*), our participation in the very life of God, *zoe*, eternal life, supernatural life, salvation, sanctification, the Kingdom of Heaven, the Kingdom of God, regeneration, the new birth, sanctifying grace, the state of grace, God's presence in the soul—these are all names for the very same thing, though they are not quite synonymous; each gives us another aspect or dimension of this "very same thing".

That life begins by faith, as its root. It grows and stretches and aspires by hope as its upward-reaching stem. It is consummated by its finest fruit and flower, love. Faith is its stuck-in-the-mud, conservative root, its anchor. Hope is its liberal, optimistic, creative, growing stem. Love is its product, its "bottom line", its proof, its point, its fruit and flower. Love *shows* faith and hope. No one can see your faith and hope except by your love.

How does this image apply to ecumenism?

Protestants emphasize the root (faith). Catholics emphasize the fruit (good works, the works of love). Faith is invisible; love is visible. Love is faith made visible. For in the New Testament, love is not an invisible feeling; love is "the works of love", as that great Protestant Kierkegaard pointed out in that great title of his.

Protestants emphasize faith, and therefore the invisible and the spiritual. For that is the indispensable beginning, that is how God gets His grace to us. Catholics emphasize the incarnational, the bodily; for that is how also God gets His grace to us: through the sacraments.

Protestants emphasize evangelism, which happens when the new believer invites the transmission of God's grace into the soul by faith, which is invisible. Catholics emphasize sacramentalism, which is the transmission of God's grace into the soul of the old believer through visible material signs. But Protestants are typically evangelized without being sacramentalized, while Catholics are typically sacramentalized without being evangelized. That is like the foundation and the building competing with each other. Protestantism inherits a big, solid foundation ("The Church's one foundation is Jesus Christ her Lord", as the hymn says) and then refuses to build anything on it except a lot of little sheds, while Catholicism is a magnificent skyscraper that has neglected its own foundation.

Obviously, something is out of whack here.

To separate the two—the material and the spiritual, body and soul—is death. Literally.

The danger in Protestantism is to have a religion that is a soul without a body. That is the ancient heresy of Gnosticism. The modern word for it is "spirituality". ("A dreadful doom", Chesterton calls it.) The danger in Catholicism is superstition, which is a kind of impersonal, automatic, mechanical materialism, like having a body without a soul. Since we *are* both body and soul (did everybody hear that shocking news?), we *need* both.

When Jesus was twelve, His Mother found Him *in the Temple*. That is the pattern. Unfortunately, too many Catholics often never find Him there (it has been happening ever since Luther's day), and that is the deepest reason why they seek Him elsewhere. And Protestants typically look for Him not in the Temple (the Church) but only in their own souls, which all too often means in their own very human feelings and experiences. Both are mistakes.

17

Do We Dare to Hope for Reunion?

Von Balthasar famously asked, in a book title, "Do we dare to hope that all men will be saved?" Part of his answer was that we are *commanded* to hope for that, and to pray for that. The prayer that Mary gave the children at Fatima was: "Lead all souls to Heaven, especially those in most need of Thy mercy." If we are to pray for it, we must hope for it. Of course, a hope is not a guarantee, and there are very strong scriptural and traditional reasons to believe that *not* all will be saved.

Similarly, we must dare to hope that Christ's broken Body may be made visibly one again for the same reason: because we are *commanded* to hope and pray for that, *because He did* (Jn 17).

John Paul II is reputed to have said that as the first millennium was the millennium of Christian unity, and the second millennium was the millennium of Christian disunity (the split with the Eastern Orthodox in 1054, then the split with Luther in 1517, then all the splits within Protestantism after that), we may hope that the third millennium may be the millennium of Christian reunification.

That would fit the universal pattern of human history, both individual and collective, the pattern that Jacques Maritain pointed to in the subtitle of one of his books: *Distinguish to Unite*. A baby is separated from its mother by being born, only so that its unity with its mother may eventually be deeper, freer, and wiser as an adult. Teenagers naturally rebel, test their wings, and fly, so that they can become freer and more complete persons and forge deeper, closer, more human and personal and adult relationships with their parents. God lets man fall from Eden so that an even more glorious unity can be attained through Christ. (Thus, Augustine famously exclaims, "O happy fault, that brought about such a great redemption!")

Yes, we not only *may* hope, but we *must* hope. And, unlike the case of von Balthasar's hope for universal salvation, we have very good reason to believe that this hope will be fulfilled. The reasons are in the very three-stage structure of our human story.

18

Sorting Out the Positives

1. We need to list, and understand, the negatives, the criticisms each church has of the other, the theological disputes, the doctrinal obstacles to reunion, and study them.

2. We need even more to list, and understand, and study, the far-deeper agreements. And we need to look at the disagreements through the lenses of the agreements, not vice versa. (That is harder to do, and therefore rarer, than we think.)

3. But I think we also need to list, and understand, the differences that are not negatives, the special gifts each side must contribute to a richer union. And it is necessary for each side to look at not only its own gifts but those of the other side, and long for them, and even envy them, as a spur to reunion.

    What they are is pretty obvious. Chapter 16 speaks of one of them: the Catholic emphasis on the bodily works of love and the Protestant emphasis on faith in the soul. There are many others, many of them accidental (yet important) and cultural (yet profitable for the whole Church), like Protestants' "hometown friendliness" and their great tradition of pre-twentieth century hymnody; Orthodox iconography and mysticism; and Catholic rational philosophy and theology.

The genius of Christianity is its ability to reconcile opposites in a "higher synthesis" that mitigates neither but perfects both—a "both-and" rather than an "either-or": supernatural and natural, unity and diversity, divinity and humanity, body and soul, grace and nature, free will and predestination, idealism and realism, individualism and communitarianism. Is Christianity so "catholic" (universal) that future generations will be able to add "Catholic and Protestant" to this list?

19

Two Ladies: A Parable

The following little parable is my friend Tom Howard's un-published invention.

A little old peasant Irish lady (let's call her Maggie) is kneel-ing before a crucifix, praying. A well-educated Protestant Evangelical lady sees her and thinks, "Poor girl, practicing Roman Catholic superstitions and praying to idols. How grateful I am that I know the Gospel! I should ask this poor lady my favorite question: Have you accepted the Lord Jesus Christ as your personal Savior?"

But suppose you could take the Protestant lady with you to the altar rail and, in her presence, ask the Catholic lady some simple questions. Real "ecumenical dialogue" may well happen—at a level far deeper than happens among scholars.

"What are you doing, Maggie?"

"Praying."

"To whom?"

"To Him." She points to Christ on the Cross.

"Who is He?"

"He's Jesus."

"And who is He?"

"He's God."

"So that's your Lord?"

"Yes."

"And what is He doing there on the Cross?"

"He's dying for me. He's saving me from my sins."

"So He's your Savior?"

"Yes."

The Protestant lady would then probably suddenly realize that the two of them were believing the same Gospel after all. They were just using different languages.

Now that's real ecumenical dialogue.

20

Jesus and Mary

Of all the distinctively Catholic beliefs, those about Mary are usually the hardest for Protestants to understand and sympathize with. Of all the Protestant objections, the objections to the Catholic teachings about Mary are usually the hardest for Catholics to understand and sympathize with.

The central key to mutual understanding here is, again, Christocentrism. Each of the Catholic teachings about Mary is centered on Christ, not on Mary. During her life on earth she was wholly relative to Him. She is *His* Mother. When the servants at the wedding at Cana wondered what to do, she pointed to Him and said, "Do whatever he tells you" (Jn 2:5). Catholics see her role as the same today. That is precisely what makes her the greatest saint: she points most completely beyond herself to Him. She is like the moon, reflecting only the sun's light (the Son's light). Her total subordination to Christ *is* her glory, and her glory *is* her total subordination to Christ. As Muslims say, she is the perfect Muslim, the perfect surrenderer.

Protestant objections to Catholic Marian doctrines are based on exactly the same principle of Christocentrism. Their premise is right (Christocentrism) even though their conclusion is wrong (that Catholics are Mariolaters, Mary idolaters). They say that Catholics raise Mary so high that she obscures Christ, like the moon eclipsing the sun. They see Catholics as worshipping her as a kind of moon goddess.

That very misunderstanding gives us hope for mutual understanding. For both sides use the same principle—one to justify Catholic Mariology, and the other to criticize it.

Catholics reply to the Protestant objection by the principle that grace perfects nature; that Christ is glorified, not obscured, by His saints; that the glory of a great king is not diminished but increased by the generosity with which he exalts his ministers; and the greatness of a good father cannot compete with or rival that of his daughter any more than the sun's glory is diminished by the moon or the artist's glory is diminished by his art.

Thus, the Catholic culture of the saints is Christ-glorifying, not Christ-detracting. Would Christ be more exalted if His saints were less—if Saint Francis of Assisi were really a playboy, or Mother Teresa a "batty old bitch", as one writer called her? Christ's glory is not like a pie that is divided up. It is infinite. He does not rival any creature. The more good, true, beautiful, and holy any creature is, the more He is exalted. For His glory is love, and love perfects and exalts the other. God is infinite generosity. If we fear that Christ's saints will obscure Christ, we are really confusing Christ with Scrooge.

Protestants reply that they do not dispute the theological principle but the pastoral practice. The moon in principle does not rival the sun, but during an eclipse it does in practice. And that is a harder thing to argue than a principle, for it requires getting inside the spiritual life of another person and making the perilous judgment whether that person's love of Mary is increasing or decreasing his love of Christ.

Who can make that judgment? Another Christian? Perhaps, but only with great trepidation and humility. God, certainly. But there is a third party who is between the two in competence: the convert. Two questions must be asked: (1) Do Protestant converts from Catholicism experience a Christian liberation from Mariolatry? Do they love Christ more because they love Mary less? And did these converts, when they were Catholics, understand the Church's teachings about Mary, or did they misunderstand and misuse them? (2) Do Catholic converts from Protestantism love Christ more because they now love Mary more? Is Mary like a surfboard that helps them ride the wave of Christ better than they could without one? And did these converts, when they were Protestants, understand the Protestant objections to Catholic Mariology correctly, or did they misunderstand them? If experience shows that one of these questions is usually answered yes more than the other, that is evidence for whichever side gives the most and strongest yes—by the use of the Christocentric principle common to both sides.

Let's also look at our common scriptural data and judge the controversial Catholic doctrines by that. Always seek a common premise when arguing about a disputed conclusion —not to ignore the disputed conclusion but to begin with its premise, its foundation. In other words, there is a logical reason for doing this, not just a personal and pragmatic reason.

Here is a major Protestant objection from scripture to Marian devotion. There is a striking paucity of scriptural data about Mary. Protestants ask: How can Mary loom so large for Catholics when she is so obscure in scripture? If we judge by quantity of revelation, quantity of data, quantity of Bible verses, Peter and Paul outrank Mary by at least ten to one.

Catholics reply that this very obscurity follows from her sanctity, from her humility, from her subordination to Christ. It does not follow necessarily, but it follows fittingly. It is not a deduction, a proof, but it is a compatibility. It is enough to answer the objection.

It is like our ignorance of why there is such evil in the world, which is the strongest argument for atheism. We simply do not know why, if God exists, He allows such great evils as the Holocaust to happen. But this ignorance on our part does not prove atheism because it is a piece of data that is quite compatible with theism as well as atheism. It is compatible with atheism because if there is no God, there is no real moral order except the one we impose, and no providential order in which good triumphs, only random chance, where "shit (evil) happens." But our inability to explain why such great evils happen is also compatible with theism because if there is a God, His wisdom must transcend ours as ours transcends a dog's, so that we would not be able to know why He tolerates evils like those that befell Job. If we knew all the answers, we would be God. We could even argue that our ability to explain all evils would prove not theism but atheism, because that would mean that there are no unexplainable mysteries and therefore no divine mind far above ours. This answer (to the problem of evil) does not prove that God exists, but it shows that the existence of evil and our inability to explain it is logically compatible with God's existence. Similarly, the paucity of data about Mary in scripture is logically compatible with both Protestant and Catholic theologies.

21

The Protestant Reformation Has Happened in the Catholic Church

Ask any serious, pious, practicing, Evangelical Protestant what the major points of his religion are. I don't mean his theology, now, the controversial *doctrines* that divide him from other Protestants as well as from Catholics, like how Christ is present in the Eucharist, or baptismal regeneration, or the authority of the creeds and the apostolic Tradition. I mean lived religious realities. How are they different for Protestants than for Catholics? If you asked Evangelicals that question, I think the following ten answers would top the list.

First and most important of all would be a Christocentrism that is personal as well as doctrinal, a lived personal relationship with Christ as Savior and Lord.

Second (though this would not be so much a formulated *object* of thought but rather a characterization or dimension *of* all their religious thought) would be the importance of the personal, the individual, the subjective. Protestants think in terms of categories like "relationship", "commitment", "daily walk", "prayer life", etc.

Third, among the objective things, scripture would take first place, and not just as an object but as a personal love and light that guides one's life, both one's inner life and outer life. Evangelicals not only know scripture—they live on it and in it. It lights up for them.

Fourth, there would be a populism, a nonclericalism, especially an expectation of lay sanctity.

Fifth, one usually finds an active, enthusiastic attitude, full of optimism and hope and love and happy friendship and fellowship. This is a hard-to-prove, vague sort of thing—it is subjective, personal, and psychological—but it is clearly discernible. And it is not Ned Flanders on *The Simpsons*.

Sixth, they have a missionary evangelism. You can't keep Christ to yourself any more than you can keep fire from spreading. Evangelicals are not afraid to be evangelical, not afraid to "witness" to the Gospel. They're not embarrassed by Christ.

Seventh, they *sing*, for the same reason.

Eighth, the spirit is more important than the letter.

Ninth, they talk, they preach. Typical Evangelical sermons are not only longer but more powerful than typical Catholic homilies.

Tenth, many of them pray long and hard and spontaneously and personally and intimately.

These are certainly ten very Christian things, not ten non-Christian things. So if Catholics are lagging behind in any or all of them, then Catholics should be imitating Evangelicals more. And in what George Weigel calls "Evangelical Catholicism", in his book by that name, they are. A quiet revolution is happening, in a general and gradual way, like a tide.

But a specific movement in the Catholic Church, vigorously approved by all the popes since Vatican II, strikingly manifests all ten of these "Evangelical" emphases. It is the Charismatic Movement. The above description fits both Protestant Evangelicalism and the Catholic Charismatic Movement to a T.

This movement either came from God or it did not. If not, it will inevitably droop and poop out, and before it does, it will do harm to the Church and individual lives. If it claims to come from God but doesn't, it is like a false prophet. But if it is of God, it will be unstoppable, and it will revitalize and renew the Catholic lives of Catholics. So look around and see what it has done, look at the facts, the data. "Come and see", and draw your own conclusions. What is God doing? The answer, you will almost always find, is that He is literally doing miracles.

This is happening much more in the global South than in the North. If you add the Catholic Charismatic Movement to Protestant Pentecostalism, both as a movement in existing Protestant denominations and in self-identified Pentecostal churches, it is the single most rapidly growing religious movement in the world. It is lighting a fire. Isn't that the main thing the Reformation tried to do in the first place?

There are many other great new movements too in the Church, but this one taps directly into the divine power source, the divine fire, the Holy Spirit. It often looks flaky and weird and embarrassing, and the charismatic style is not everybody's personal style (e.g., it is not mine), just as Gregorian chant and Gothic cathedrals and medieval philosophy are not everybody's style (as they are mine). But it is a work of God. And it is healing divisions, especially in the Catholic Church.

22

A Little Comic Relief

During the troubles in Northern Ireland, a man was out late walking in the dark. Suddenly there was an arm around his neck and a knife to his throat. "Tell me true if ye want to live: are ye a Protestant or are ye a Catholic?"

The man thought quickly. He had a 50 percent chance to live. That seemed too little. So he replied, "I'm an atheist."

The knife did not move. "Are ye a Protestant atheist or a Catholic atheist?"

There are still places in the world where the difference between a Protestant and a Catholic is more severe than the difference between a Christian and an atheist.

23

Sorting Things Out among Converts and Their Motives

In order to get to the point, I first have to back up and set up a structure in the soul.

Three factors determine the goodness or evil of any human act: the act itself, the motive, and the circumstances (including consequences). All three count; all three must be good for the deed to be good. But motive is the most important factor in making choices, because motive reveals character. Motives are the heart of the matter because they come from the heart. Motive shapes character, and character is destiny, character is eternal. As Saint Augustine says, you are what you love, you become what you love; therefore, your motives, which come from your loves, not only reveal your self but also make your self, constitute your self. And your self is eternal.

There are three good motives for religious choices, corresponding to the three "theological virtues", i.e., faith, hope, and charity.

These correspond to the three deepest human desires: truth, joy (which is our response to beauty, especially spiritual beauty), and goodness. They are three attributes of God and therefore three things everyone instinctively wants, and wants without limit and absolutely. This is why there are three things that distinguish man from the beast, three signatures of the human soul: reason, art, and morality.

This is why there are three protagonists in most great epics—because there are these three powers of the human soul, which nearly all psychologists, from Plato to Freud, have recognized: the mind; the heart, or desires; and the moral will. We always find a prophet, a priest, and a king; an intellectual, a humble, practical servant, and a strong-willed ruler. Thus Gandalf, Frodo, and Aragorn. Thus Ivan, Alyosha, and Dmitri Karamazov. Thus Mr. Spock, "Bones" McCoy, and Captain Kirk in *Star Trek*. Thus Hooper, Brodie, and Quint in *Jaws*. Thus John, James, and Peter in the Gospels, Jesus' "inner circle". There are always three.

The first of the human needs, and prerequisite to all others, is truth. The only good and honest reason for faith in anything is the thing's truth. Even goodness and joy cannot trump truth, for they must be *true* goodness and *true* joy. Faith in Santa Claus gave you greater joy and even greater goodness (moral behavior) every Christmas when you were very young, but you were right to abandon that faith. Why? For one reason only, the only one that could ever trump joy and goodness: truth.

A long but necessary digression about defining our terms:

Just as "reason" can be used in the ancient, broader sense as including intuition as well as reasoning, so "heart" can be used in a broader, ancient, scriptural sense rather than in a narrower, modern, merely emotional and subjective sense. The "heart" can mean at least three different things:

1. The prefunctional root of all three of these distinctively human functions or faculties or powers of intellect, emotions, and will; the nonobjectifiable "I"-subject behind all distinctively human acts of faith, hope, and love.

2. That power in the soul from which emerges love and thus determines my destiny ("Amor meus, pondus meum", says Augustine: "My love is my weight, my gravity"). This includes will. Love is essentially an act of will, the will to the good of another.

3. That power in us that feels and emotes. This is a narrower, more modern sense.

   Some of these feelings are much less important than we think they are—and are to be ignored (as all the saints say, scandalizing our contemporary culture, which fondles feelings as if they were rosary beads). But some of them are more substantive and essential and "true", e.g., when we feel rightly *about* some good *because* it is good; or when we feel a cosmic gratitude, or great compassion. This is what some call the "eye of the heart"—e.g., Pascal, who famously says that the heart has its "reasons". It is from these deeper feelings of the heart, as well as from the deliberate will, that emerge what Dietrich von Hildebrand calls "value responses". (I highly recommend his little book *The Heart*, especially to people who tend to be too much like Stoics or "cold fish" rationalists.)

Christ fulfills all three of these needs and values. He is "the way, and the truth, and the life" (Jn 14:6). (1) He is the way to joy, the way of salvation, the way to Heaven, the way to the Father. (2) He is "the truth", for truth is conformity to reality, and He is perfect conformity to the ultimate reality, the ultimate truth, the mind of God, the being of God. He comes into this world not to teach His own mind but the mind of the Father (Jn 7:16). (3) He is also "the life", the life of love, of goodness, of sanctity, of conformity to the will of God. He comes into this world not to do His own will but the will of His Father (Jn 4:34). That is the heart of morality, of goodness, of sanctity.

Therefore, saying yes to all three of these values—beauty (joy), truth, and goodness (love)—are ways of saying yes to Christ, in objective fact, whether one subjectively knows one is assenting to Christ or not. Whenever we seek these three divine things, the true and the good and the beautiful, what we are seeking is really Christ.

Now, in light of this, let us look at the Protestant-Catholic issue. Let us look at it from the point of view of eight differ-ent people who make four different choices between these two churches for two different motives. (It is really much less complicated than it sounds.)

Person 1 is born Catholic and stays Catholic for the right motive, i.e. for Christ (in at least one of His three aspects: the way of salvation, the truth of being, or the life of love).

Person 2 is born Catholic and becomes Protestant for the same motive, i.e., for Christ (in at least one of these three ways).

Person 3 is born Protestant and stays Protestant for Christ.

Person 4 is born Protestant and becomes Catholic for Christ.

Person 5 is born Catholic and stays Catholic but for a motive other than Christ.

Person 6 is born Catholic and becomes Protestant but for a motive other than Christ.

Person 7 is born Protestant and stays Protestant but for a motive other than Christ.

Person 8 is born Protestant and becomes Catholic but for a motive other than Christ.

We all know, by hearsay if not by experience, all eight of these people. In fact, each person reading this book is probably one of them.

However, we may be mistaken, even about ourselves, regarding our deepest motive: do we select the church we select for Christ's sake, do we see this choice in terms of Christ? Or do we see Christ in terms of some other thing (any other thing) in the church that we embrace or in the church that we reject?

Do we choose Catholicism because we seek the most total, most perfect, and most intimate relationship with Christ possible and because we believe Christ is really present in the Eucharist and as the author behind the Church's authoritative teachings, even those teachings that challenge our minds and correct our desires and demand obedience from our wills? Or do we choose Catholicism because it makes us feel good, or because it is easier, or because it is older or bigger, or because it is newer or smaller, or because it is smarter (not the same thing as "wiser"), or maybe even because it is prettier?

Do we choose Protestantism because we seek the most-intimate-possible relationship with Christ, or do we choose it because we are reacting against the dullness and sinfulness of Catholics or because we would rather not toe the Church's line on sexual morality, or because it is newer and spiffier and simpler, or because we like the fellowship, the friends, perhaps even the music better?

One church must be right and the other must be wrong, it seems, at least on issues like transubstantiation and papal infallibility and *sola scriptura* and Marian dogmas. These are either-ors. It is terribly important to know the objective truth about God and His will for us. But it is also terribly important to have the right human will, the right motive. That much, at least, we can know of God's will: what motives He wants us to have. We do not agree about what church He wants us to join, but we do agree on what motive He wants us to have for deciding what church to join. So we all, Protestants and Catholics alike, approve the first four of these eight choices more than the last four.

There are various ways of dividing these eight people into two groups of four each: Catholics versus Protestants is only one of them. Those who choose to change and those who do not is another division of four against four. But the most important division, *from Christ's point of view* (and is there a better one?), is the division by motive. He has promised us that if our will's motive is straightened out, our knowledge will get straightened out too, in His time and in His way. "Seek, and you will find" (see Mt 7:7). "If any man's will is to do his [the Father's] will, he shall know whether the teaching is from God" (Jn 7:17).

When we try to sort out these eight cases, we try to do so from a God's-eye point of view, of course; and since that is the point of view of omniscience, we naturally think that that point of view is like that of an author over all his characters, since God, like an author, designed and invented and created all His characters. This is true, but what we tend to forget is that God's point of view is *not from outside but from inside*, from inside each character, in fact from the heart of each character, and even from the center of the heart, from the heart of the heart. Remember Saint Augustine's answer to the question "Where is God?": "He is more present to me than I am to myself." That is why motive is so important.

But—since motive is so important—we have to be careful of our own motives in working for ecumenism. Reunion will not be attained if we work for it as our end, our fundamental motive; for that is idolatry. There is no God but God. Only God is our end; God will not let Himself be instrumentalized, used as a means to attain any other end, however good it may be. That is a kind of idolatry.

We are constantly tempted to all kinds of hidden idolatries, tempted to put second things first and first things second. That is why God has to do much of His work indirectly. He can't answer our stupid prayers, only our wise ones, because He is not stupid. The one prayer He always answers is "Thy will be done."

So the surest way to reunion is to love God more than we love reunion, and to love reunion only because we love God.

∼

God is truth, so truth is absolute. But God is not ecclesiastical organization, so that is not absolute—that is relative and therefore negotiable. Surprisingly negotiable, perhaps, to many Catholics. The divine authority of the Church is nonnegotiable and unchangeable, since it is from God; but the structures of authority *in* the Church are changeable, since they are from men, even though they were holy men. In fact, these structures have changed considerably throughout the Church's history. The primacy of the Bishop of

Rome as the successor of Saint Peter has always been there, but it has been expressed differently in different times. That is why John Paul II said that those structures of authority can and should continue to find different and better expressions, especially in dialogue with the Eastern Orthodox.

But of course, a change in expressing something cannot be a change in the substance of that something, for then it would no longer be a change in expressing *that* something.

A famous formula for dealing with differences in the Church is "In essentials, unity; in nonessentials, diversity; in all things, charity." All three parts are necessary. To compromise essentials is a betrayal of truth. To refuse to compromise nonessentials is pigheaded Phariseeism. To compromise charity is to compromise Christ.

And what impedes our obedience to these three parts of the formula is always our motives, our hearts. Our hearts instruct or blind our heads. That is why orthopraxy (right practice) must lead and instruct orthodoxy (right belief). Remember John 7:17.

To compromise truth for the sake of love, e.g., to compromise essentials for the sake of better relations between the churches, is *not* to have a good motive, even if it is done for love; for it must be done for love of God, and God is truth, so we can never ignore truth.

To refuse to change or compromise nonessentials for the sake of truth is not to have a good motive either, even if it is done for truth, for it must be done for God, and God is love, so we may never ignore love.

To hold fast to essentials and to grant freedom in nonssentials for any other motive than the love of both the true and the good, is to do the right thing for the wrong reason, and that bad motive will pollute even good deeds.

So it is not that easy to obey the formulation. It is like the Ten Commandments: very easy to understand, very hard to obey. Most of the work of ecumenism has been focused on the understanding, the scholarship. That is necessary, and let it continue. But more of the work must be focused on the obeying. If we all became brilliant theologians (a consummation devoutly to be wished), reunion would still be far away. If we all became saints, it would be at our doorstep.

24

Sorting Out the Issues in "Comparative Religions"

All religions contain three aspects or dimensions, corresponding to the three powers of the image of God in the soul—the three powers that raise us above the animals, the three powers that chapter 23 was about: mind, will, and heart ("heart" can be interpreted as emotion, or imagination, or creativity—that third thing is much harder to pin down). Every religion has a creed, a code, and a cult (i.e., a liturgy). Every religion includes words, works, and worship. They seek the true (creed), the good (code), and the beautiful (cult).

There are three answers to the "problem of comparative religions", i.e., how to compare the religions of the world. "Exclusivism" contends that there are irreconcilable contradictions between any two religions, and they can't both be right. "Inclusivism" contends that deep down all religions are saying the same thing, or at least things that are not incompatible and irreconcilable, and we could see this if only we could get the "deep-down" or mystical perspective. And "pluralism" says that the different religions are simply different, like cats and dogs, or different styles of music.

When we evaluate these three options in the second paragraph by distinguishing the three aspects or dimensions in the first paragraph, we find that exclusivism seems to be right about creeds, inclusivism seems to be right about codes, and pluralism seems to be right about cults.

Almost all the problems in interreligious dialogue are in the first area: creeds, beliefs, truth-claims. There is little problem in the second area: there is massive (though not quite total) agreement among all the religions of the world regarding morality. And there is little problem in the third area because every religion already fosters pluralism within itself in approving diverse modes of public worship and personal devotion, though some (like Hinduism, with its four very different yogas) go further than others (like Islam, with its "five pillars" that are obligatory for everyone).

But Christ is not confined to any one of these three areas or dimensions. We cannot even say that He is present *primarily* in only one. He is the fulfillment of all three: He is "the way, and the truth, and the life" (Jn 14:6). Therefore, the choice for or against Christ is a more primordial choice, a more eternally momentous choice, than any merely doctrinal, merely moral, or merely liturgical, devotional, or ecclesiastical choice. And that is why the motive, the heart's "fundamental option", is the single most important thing.

What is true of interfaith dialogue (between Christians and non-Christians) is also for the most part true of ecumenical dialogue (between different types of Christians, especially Protestants and Catholics). One great use of interfaith dialogue is to give us a sense of perspective, so that we can see that the differences between Protestants and Catholics, while serious, are incomparably less than the differences between all Christians and all non-Christians—or, positively put, that what unites us is massively more than what divides us. We would not see this if there were no other religious options in the world. Similarly, dialogue with atheists gives us the perspective to see that the differences among the world's religions, while great, are incomparably less than the differences between atheism and theism.

However, this pattern or outline of increasing and decreasing differences does not extend to the differences within Protestantism. For the differences between "conservative" or "traditional" or "Evangelical" or "Biblical" Protestants and "liberal" or "modernist" Protestants is far greater than the differences between orthodox Protestants and orthodox Catholics. Modernist or liberal Christians do not even believe in the supernatural, in the miraculous, and therefore in the Incarnation and the deity of Christ. From the Catholic point of view, Eastern Orthodoxy is in schism, and Reformation Protestantism is in heresy, but liberal or modernist Protestantism is in apostasy. (Incidentally, a number of media-famous "Catholic" theologians teach this modernism!) Biblical Protestants have far more in common with believing Catholics than with the modernists in their own denominations. For whether Christ is divine is incomparably more important than whether He authorized the visible Catholic Church. Who Christ is, is incomparably more important than who the pope is. Whether Christ came down from Heaven is incomparably more important than whether Mary was assumed into Heaven.

Flannery O'Connor, the great Catholic novelist, lived in the South, the "Bible Belt". She shocked her largely Baptist audience when she said to them that she was closer to them than to some theologians in her own Catholic Church and that they were closer to the pope than they were to some of the theologians in the liberal fringes of their own denomination. This was in the fifties. Very few are shocked anymore. That fact means that great progress in understanding, in perspective, in seeing things as they are, has been made in the last seventy years.

25

Names

Names mean something. Always.

What does "Protestant" mean? It means "protesting". Protestants protest against something: either against abuses and corruptions in the Catholic Church or against the Catholic Church herself. Luther was in the first category; most Protestants today are in the second category: they do not expect "Protestantism" to disappear, ever.

In both cases, "Protestant" is a relative term. It is relative to what is being protested against. And that is the Catholic Church.

What does "Catholic" mean? It means "universal". The Catholic Church claims to embrace, to include, many things, as well as many peoples. Perhaps it is "catholic" enough to include Protestant things. (I deliberately use "things" in the broadest, most undefined sense. My point is merely linguistic, not theological.) Its spirit is to include, not to exclude; to affirm, not to protest against, as much as possible. Its "yesses" far outweigh its "nos". In fact, all its "nos" are for the sake of its "yesses".

Of course, sometimes protest is right and inclusion is wrong. The martyrs protested paganism, and Bonhoeffer protested Nazism, and Solzhenitsyn protested Communism.

And they were right not to be "catholic" and inclusive and collaborationist with evil.

But they didn't make a religion out of "martyrism" or "Bonhoefferism" or "anti-communism."

If the Catholic Church were to disappear (which cannot happen in the real world but which can happen in thought), Protestantism would disappear too, for what would Protestants protest against? What identity would an anti-Communist have if Communism disappeared?

How much of a revolution would it be if we all thought positively instead of negatively?

26

Historical Perspectives
(from the Future) on the Reformation

How will Catholic historians one thousand years from now
view the Reformation?

Will they view it as a simple revolt against the Church,
as Catholics have argued, or as a necessary reform of the
Church that the Church resisted and excluded, as Protestants have argued? I think it will be viewed as something in
between these two, as an unfortunate (Catholics are right
there) but necessary (Protestants are right there) event in
the history of the Church, as something like a rebellious
teenager running away from a home that has become seri-
ously dysfunctional. He is still part of the family, and there
must eventually be a reconciliation.

After all, the Church calls Protestants not only "*separated*
brethren" but "separated *brethren*". The "brethren" part is
more salient than the "separated" part. The noun outweighs
the adjective. That teenager is our own kid. And when he
comes back home (and it is his home: home is not defined
by your end but by your beginning, your origin, your roots,
your parents), he will find it different. It will have cleaned
up much of the poop that is inevitable on Noah's ark.

But not all of it. Remember the profound children's book

title *Everybody Poops*. Poop is a divinely designed symbol of Original Sin. Even if there is food in Heaven, there won't be poop. (Don't ask me how God might pull that off; just remember that He invented giraffes and pufferfish.)

When Luther returns to Rome, he will not have to write another ninety-five theses, or another *Christian Liberty*. Those protests will have been taken care of. But the animals on the ark cannot become angels, and he will still have to help clean up a lot of other poop, though not dogmatic poop. (There is none of that if the dogmas that the Church insists are divine revelation are indeed divine revelation. And if the Church is wrong there, we had better all become Protestants immediately.) He will not find Noah's descendants, who man the ark, perfect people; but he will find them dysfunctional in different ways than he did in 1517.

Above all, he will find it his home. The lamp has been kept burning in the window. You can see that lamp in any Catholic church. It is the little red sanctuary lamp next to the Tabernacle where the Host is kept. It tells you Who is waiting there for you.

Even when the son says, "That's not my mother anymore!" the mother does not say, "That's not my son anymore." She says, "That is my runaway son, and he will come home because he belongs here—because this is his home and I am his mother, no matter what he says."

27

What Will Make Good Protestants Come Home?

Good Protestants are those committed to the best thing in Protestantism, the thing that justified Luther, in his own mind, in the radical act of leaving the Church, the one and only Church that had existed since Christ's own day, and becoming the first "Protestant", as distinct from just another reformer like Saint Francis of Assisi or Saint Bernard of Clairvaux.

But though he left Rome rather than reform it (and that was the fault of stubborn, sinful churchmen on both sides), Luther did *not* want to build a new church. That cannot be done, and he understood that. That would be a radically un-Christian enterprise. He wanted to reform the Church, to purify her; but he wanted to reform or purify or restore not merely some of her bad accidents and corruptions, like the sale of indulgences. He wanted to reform the fact that most Catholics did not know the Gospel. They didn't know how to get to Heaven. They were like my students at Boston College. They didn't know Jesus Christ even though they knew *about* him.

Let's call that "best thing" in Protestantism, the reason Luther left, the "Evangelical Principle".

When Catholics learn this principle, many, many Protestants will come home.

For this is not just the heart and essence of Luther's reformation—it is *God's* reformation. Therefore, it will succeed. Protestants' greatest concern and love and care and ambition will succeed. The Reformation will succeed. When? Not when the Church abandons any of her from-the-beginning traditional dogmatic or moral or sacramental or ecclesial theological dogmas, which are her divinely delivered data. She will never do that. But the Protestant Reformation will succeed when Catholics remember their center, their essence, their "first love" (see Rev 2:4). When more than just a minority of Catholics remember their first love, more than just a minority of Protestants will come home. And then both "sides" will "win".

It is beginning to happen. The tide has turned.

Note on the Next Few Chapters

A few of Pascal's *Pensées* (about ten) are long and finished essays, while the others (about nine hundred) are short notes. I therefore deliberately do much the same thing: after the above twenty-seven short notes, I continue with five longer chapters on five important dimensions of the issue: Mary, evangelism, ecumenism, ecclesiology, and hermeneutics (Biblical interpretation).

28

Mary

When Protestants hear the Catholic term "Mariology", they immediately think "Mariolatry". "Mariolatry" means "the idolatry of Mary", which means literally "the worship of Mary as God". Most Protestants do not believe that most Catholics literally worship Mary as God, but they think that Catholics come dangerously close to it.

"Mariolatry" is a question-begging term. It does not describe; it accuses. But "Mariology" is a perfectly innocent and neutral term. It means "the science of Mary".

"Science" is used here in the broad, ancient sense, i.e., any rational study—not in the narrow, modern sense, i.e., the scientific method. Thus, philosophy and theology are sciences in the ancient sense, though not in the modern sense. As some of the subdivisions of philosophy are metaphysics (the philosophy of being), epistemology (the philosophy of knowing), and political philosophy, so some of the subdivisions of Christian theology are ecclesiology (the theology of the Church), the "theology of the body", and Mariology (the theology of Mary).

This science, like others (e.g., ethics, logic, economics, and military science) has two parts: "theoretical" or "speculative", and "practical". "Theoretical" and "speculative" do not mean "uncertain". They mean "the search for truth for its own sake, simply to know it, to understand it, to contemplate it". Thus, these sciences are also called "contemplative", as distinct from "active". And "practical" means not "efficient" but "the search for truth for the sake of action, for the sake of putting it into practice". Most sciences have these two parts, for they include both principles and also practical applications of them.

In the case of Mariology, the principles are the doctrinal beliefs. Some of these are revealed dogmas, including the two that Protestants object to the most strongly, i.e., Mary's Assumption into Heaven (like that of Enoch and Elijah) and her Immaculate Conception (her being conceived in her mother's womb without Original Sin, by a divine miracle). And some of the principles of Mariology are beliefs inherent in titles that the Church has officially and authoritatively given to her, such as the "second Eve" and the "Mother of God". The practices are private and public devotions and prayers, such as the Hail Mary, which are based on the theological principles. For instance, Catholics "hail" Mary, in their prayers, for the same reason the angel did in scripture: because she is "full of grace" (Lk 1:28).

Protestants object to both sides of Catholic Mariology, the principles and the practices, on the basis of *sola scriptura*: they are not explicitly in scripture. Catholics reply that their historical foundation is there in the scriptural data, just as it is for the doctrine of the Trinity. In the case of the Trinity, the scriptural data are that (1) God is one, (2) the Father is God, (3) the Son is God, (4) the Holy Spirit is God, (5) the Father is not the Son—they are distinct persons, (6) the Son is not the Holy Spirit—they are distinct persons, and

(7) the Father is not the Holy Spirit—they are distinct persons.

The same principle applies to Purgatory, by the way. Here, the scriptural data are that (1) perfect holiness and sin are incompatible opposites, (2) in Heaven there is perfect holiness and nothing sinful, and (3) in this world we are still sinners, with sinful habits and desires. Catholics argue that Protestants must deny or minimize one of these three pieces of scriptural data if they deny Purgatory.

Most Protestants find Catholic Mariology, both the theological principles and the devotional practices, the single most objectionable thing about the Catholic Church. Catholics don't understand this. They feel about Protestant attacks on their Marian doctrines and devotions the same way a loyal son feels about attacks on his mother. But most Evangelical Protestants who become Catholics say that (1) the Marian doctrines were the last and hardest obstacle they had to overcome, and (2) this obstacle lingered in their feelings, if not their beliefs, for quite a while even while they were Catholics—it took them many years as Catholics to understand and appreciate the Catholic devotion to Mary. (3) Yet when they do finally come fully to share Catholics' enthusiasm and love for Marian doctrines and devotions, they say that now they simply cannot understand their former attitude, how they could have missed and misunderstood Catholic Mariology. This psychological change is not only a puzzle, but a puzzle even to those who have solved it by swimming across the Tiber!

Here is a possible clue.

I was once talking about ecumenism to an audience composed equally of Protestants and Catholics. Both "sides" loved each other, and loved Jesus Christ, and loved the idea of learning from each other and working for ecumenical unity. Everything I had said up to then, even things that were more Catholic than Protestant, had produced nods of agreement from all. This included theological points like the Catholic doctrine that divine grace raises up and perfects everything in nature rather than demeans it, and that therefore, in principle, to exalt Mary is not to demean God any more than to exalt God is to demean Mary. The Protestants agreed with this principle, though not with the way Catholics applied it to Mary. We were still in the atmosphere of convivial ecumenism, even though we were talking about the issue that most divided us, because we were talking about it theoretically. But when I opined that Mary, who seemed the biggest obstacle to ecumenism, would prove to be the biggest *cause* of it through her passionate prayers to our common Lord for unity among His and her spiritual children—when I said this, you could hear a pin drop.

Sometimes you can *see or hear* deep states of heart and soul—when you hear people stop breathing, or when you see facial changes. I could see most of the Protestants furrowing their brows with surprise, while I could see most of the Catholics smiling a knowing "of course". *There* was the real fissure that divided us. It was not theological arguments about her so much as the possibility of her real intervention, her real presence. That had become clear when I suddenly changed my point of view from the former to the latter. Ironically, when I was talking about how our beliefs about Mary divided us, we were not as deeply divided as when I was discussing how Mary herself would unite us— not because I was talking about union rather than division but because I was talking about *her* rather than about our talk about her.

Protestantism began in 1517. We are remembering the five hundredth anniversary of this event in 2017. Mary's most important and famous and widely seen appearance in history[1] was probably the one at Fatima, in 1917. We will also celebrate the one hundredth anniversary of this event in 2017. The numbers may be a mere coincidence, but divine providence rules all things, including numbers. There are probably many, many more connections between historical events from Heaven's point of view than there are from ours. "There are more things in heaven and earth than are dreamt of in your philosophy."

The Protestants in my audience were thinking not of Mary herself but of the Catholic Church's Marian *dogmas* and *practices*. And they were, of course, looking at them from without, since they did not believe or practice them. The Catholics, in contrast, were looking at them from within, from experience. But that experience was the experience of the interpersonal relationship they had with her, a relationship of faith, hope, love, and prayer. When I said that she would be a *cause* of reunion, I was not thinking mainly of agreement about a definition, a doctrine, a propositional truth. I was thinking of her as a real cause, a real power, a real person who answered our prayers. (Aristotle would call that an efficient cause, not just a formal cause or a final

---

[1] The one exception would be her appearances at Zeitoun, outside Cairo, Egypt, in 1968, where Mary appeared on the dome of an Orthodox cathedral to two million Muslims and Christians, making peace signs, calling for another reconciliation among her spiritual children and one potentially even more momentous.

cause.) Doctrines may be true and practices may be good, but only persons can answer prayers.

How can Mary herself unite us even while the Catholic Marian doctrines and practices separate us? I think there is a very important parallel case to this one that has a similar puzzle and a similar solution. Imagine an audience composed of honest, loving, open-minded Christians and Muslims. Imagine the Christian speaker making a statement about Jesus' fundamental distinctive claim, which Muslims disbelieve and even find blasphemous—the claim to be the one and only way to God: "I am the way, and the truth, and the life; no one comes to the Father, but by me" (Jn 14:6). Suppose the Christian tries to explain that according to the teachings of the Church this does not mean that Muslims cannot know or love God or go to Heaven. But it means that if and when they do, it is, in objective, ontological fact, only by means of Christ, whether they know this or not. For Christ is "the true light that enlightens *every man*" (Jn 1:9; emphasis added). Jesus Himself will get these non-Christians to Heaven. The Christian thinks this is an ecumenical and liberal gesture. But the Muslim not only disagrees but gets his hackles up, feels insulted. He feels that this attempt at openhanded acceptance really opens the gap between Christians and Muslims rather than closes it. Why?

It is because the Christian's explanation is about reality, about a real Person, not just about a theological or moral belief. At first, the two of them were discussing different doctrines. They disagreed, in a fundamental and nonnegotiable way; but this was expected and not offensive or surprising to either side. It was safe because both sides were at a safe distance from the real Christ. They may have tried to compare their different theologies of Christ by setting out agreements and disagreements in two columns; and they might have found many more agreements than disagreements. Practically, both revered Christ as holy. Theologically, they found that the Christ of the Qur'an is a pretty thick slice of the Christ of the New Testament. In the Qur'an too he was a prophet of the one true God, spoke the true Gospel, was the promised Messiah, was virgin born, performed miracles, raised the dead, was sinless, and will return to judge the whole world at the end of time.

But all this comfortable togetherness would change when the Christian says, in effect, that the real Jesus is the Person who is even now enabling them to know and love God as good Muslims, and who will be their only entrance ticket to Heaven. Now they are no longer discussing a portrait but touching a Person. It is like finding the rock you are stepping on turning into an alligator: "Look out! It's alive!" Because the Muslims had been objective about the portrait, and somewhat intellectually detached from it, they had been able somewhat to understand and imaginatively enter into the Christian's theology even though they emphatically did not believe its central claim, that Christ is not just a man but the eternal Son of God. But now the Christian says that this Person is alive and acting here and now, and actually causing (or being the Father's universal instrumental cause for) all the good in the world, including the good that is presently happening in them, in their wisdom and good will; that all the good they can personally hope for in eternity will in fact come to them through Him; and that He is their only hope to receive what they already know is their only hope of salvation, i.e., Allah's mercy. Now we're in a whole new dimension: this is religion instead of theology.

To remember the difference, remember C. S. Lewis' joke about the theologian who, at the gate of Heaven, was given by God the choice between going into Heaven or going to a theology lecture on Heaven. He chose the lecture.

The parallel between the way Catholic beliefs about Mary are most threatening to Protestants and the way Christian beliefs about Christ are most threatening to Muslims is not perfect. Obviously, Mary is not, like Christ, personally responsible for all the good in the world. But she is responsible for being the "perfect Muslim", the perfect surrenderer, whose Yes ("fiat"—"Let it be to me according to your word" [Lk 1:38]) alone brought to us Him through whom alone we have knowledge of God, divine grace, and the hope of salvation.

~

Let's look at the same thing again. (That simple technique, rare among us impatient moderns, often turns up more new insights than you thought it would.)

Protestants are not threatened by anything in the Bible, including Mary. But they are threatened by the suspicion that Catholics succumb to myth and exaggeration about her, and even idolatry. Educated Protestants don't usually say or believe that Catholics literally worship and adore Mary as God; but when they look at all the honorific titles the Church gives to her—"cause of our joy", "queen of Heaven", "Mother of God", "immaculate", "our life, our sweetness, and our hope"—they think they see more love and attention lavished on her than on Christ. They hear more "Hail Marys" than "Hail Christs". They may admit that Mary is indeed beautiful, like the moon—but the moon seems to be eclipsing the Son on the Catholic side of the world.

Catholics reply that that is impossible both in practice and in theory: in practice, because every Hail Mary *is* a Hail Christ, a petition for her *to petition Christ*; and in theory, because all the Marian dogmas are Christocentric, not Mary-centric. The title "Mother of God" was given to Mary in order to defend Christ's full divinity against those who denied it. The controversy was not so much about her as about Him.

Catholics are thus deeply puzzled by the Protestant objection, for it seems to presuppose a very bad theological principle: that grace and nature, God and man, are rivals; that their glory is like pieces of a pizza: the more pieces one has, the fewer the other has. How can the glory of a great king be dimmed by the fact that he generously shares his glory with his subordinates? Is God in competition with His creatures? Would Christ be greater if His saints were less? If Saint Francis of Assisi were only a hippie pothead, would that glorify Christ more? If God chose to fill Mary with even more grace than any other saint, to make her "full of grace", as full as any merely human being ever was, how does that diminish Christ? It is for Christ's glory (and also *from* Christ's glory) that God does that. And it is only through Christ's mediation that God does that. (There are no other real channels of grace, no channels that bypass Christ.)

Christ's glory is not like a pizza, with a finite number of slices that diminish when divided up and given out. It is infinite. He no more rivals any creature than light rivals any color. The more good and true and beautiful any creature is, the more Christ is glorified. And the reason for this is that His glory is charity, and charity exalts and perfects all its objects. That is why "grace perfects nature": because "God is love" (1 Jn 4:8). God has absolutely no ego problem. He is offended by our sins not because they harm Him (impossible!) but only because they harm us. So if we fear that the saints will rival Christ, we are confusing Christ with Scrooge. Christ didn't hold anything back: the Incarnation is total (He is "like us in all things but sin" [Heb 4:15, KJV]). And His generosity is total: although one drop of His blood would have been enough to save the world, He gave us twelve pints, on the Cross, because he had twelve pints to give. He literally and physically "emptied himself" (Phil 2:7) for us. The answer to those who object to the Marian doctrines is Christ, as described in Philippians 2:5–11.

Why don't Protestants see in Mary what the Church sees? It is because they have not meditated deeply on Philippians 2:5–11. They don't appreciate Mary's holiness because they don't appreciate Christ's holiness deeply enough. Jesus did not see His divinity as a thing to be "grasped" (Phil 2:6) and jealously kept, greedily hoarded. That would be confusing Christ with a dragon. That would be confusing Christ with one of the seven deadly sins, envy—envy of another's good, envy of the good shared with another. That would be confusing Christ with Dracula. Dracula takes our blood; Christ gives us His. Salvation is a blood transfusion.

What explains the glory the Church sees in Mary? Two things: pure generosity on Christ's part, and pure humility and submission and surrender on Mary's part.

Muslims understand that and exalt her total "surrender" to God. She is "the perfect Muslim", the perfect surren-derer. Her glory, her exaltation, is precisely her total subordination. What is most exalted is what most humbles itself. This is what she said in her "Magnificat", and Christ said the exact same thing in His sermons thirty years later. When I compare Muslim devotion to Mary with Protestant suspicions, I sometimes think some pious Muslims understand the spirit of Christ better than some Christians do.

Even Buddhists see selfish "grasping" (*tanha*) as the root of all evil and suffering. Sometimes I think pious Buddhists understand the spirit of Christ better than some Christians do.

~

Why does the Church exalt Mary so? Because God did. Because God's angel did. And why does she deserve the angel's title "full of grace"? Because she really was full of grace! It's not a stretch, it's a "duh"! She was "wholly borne by God's grace" like a surfer on a wave.[2]

Christ gave us Mary three times: (1) by His eternal divine providence, to be the free channel by which He would come into the world to save us; (2) at the end of His life, from the Cross ("Behold, your mother!" [Jn 19:27]); and (3) through His Church's ongoing meditation on and unpacking of this mystery.

And Mary gave us Christ three times: (1) by freely consenting to bear Him, at the Annunciation; (2) by sharing in His life and His sufferings (see the movie *The Passion of the Christ* again); and (3) by continually interceding with Him for us. As she brought Christ down to us in the Incarnation,

[2] *Catechism of the Catholic Church*, 2nd ed. (Vatican City: Libreria Editrice Vaticana; Washington, D.C.: United States Catholic Conference, 2000), 490 (hereafter cited as *CCC*).

as His door into our world, she continues to bring Christ's graces down to us by her intercessory prayers. It is what mothers do. And it is what prayer does. As Pascal said, God instituted prayer in order to graciously give His creatures the dignity of being active causes, free cooperators with His grace. For grace turns nature on, not off—especially human nature, and most especially human nature's free will. Grace and free will are not rivals; in fact, they can marry and allow miracles to happen, as man and woman become one flesh and allow the miracle of a new person to happen.

And because God's grace turns on our free will rather than turning it off, Mary being full of grace means that Mary fully and freely wills and chooses grace, loves God with her whole heart and soul and mind and strength, actively obeys the first and greatest commandment. Her surrender to His grace is not passive but active because grace perfects the activities of human nature.

Nothing is more Biblical than the historical fact that in God's providential plan, it was her free surrender to His will, her "Let it be to me according to your word", that made our salvation possible. (For that "word" is not just four Hebrew letters—it is one divine Person.)

If Mary had said no, Christ would not have come. He spiritually seduces but does not rape. He Himself made His coming dependent on her choice. Thus, indirectly but really, she is a link in the chain of our salvation, in fact the link that most directly connects us with Christ. In this sense, she is our active "co-operator in redemption" by her fiat. This is what is meant by the threatening-sounding term "co-redemptrix". There is also a second sense in which she is co-redemptrix: she also actively prays for our salvation now, as we pray for each other's; and she, like us, "operates-with" the Savior, or *co*-operates in salvation—*as every Christian does*, though she does it more perfectly.

God did that, not the Church. The Church only ponders (as Mary "pondered"; see Lk 2:19) what the Bible says God did, just as the Church "pondered" the Trinity and the two natures of Christ in the first six centuries, and the sacraments in the Middle Ages, and social ethics in modern times. The Church, like Mary, does not discover new truths, new dogmas; nor does she merely deduce consequences logically from old truths; instead, she continually ponders and explores and unpacks her "deposit of faith", which she calls Sacred Tradition, of which the Bible is the most important part. Mary is not only an important part of that deposit but also the model, in her "pondering", of what the Church does with it.

～

Let's "ponder" this—i.e., let's go through it again, even though we went through it before, because it is not just an abstract idea that we either understand or don't, and either accept or reject, but something we have to look at again and again, more and more, like a human face.

There are two unanswerable reasons why the Church's Marian dogmas augment Christ's glory rather than rival or diminish it. These two reasons are not theological arguments but historical facts. They are that (1) Christ gave us Mary, and (2) Mary gave us Christ.

Christ gave us Mary first in His Incarnation, by providentially raising her up to be His Mother. He is the only man who ever lived who chose His own Mother! Second, Christ gave us Mary personally from the Cross, when He said to

John, the only disciple who remained faithful to Him to the end, "Behold, your mother!" and to His Mother, "Behold, your son!" (Jn 19:27, 26). Christ gave us Mary a third time through the Church that He deliberately created and authorized. "He who hears you hears me" (Lk 10:16), He said to His chosen Apostles, who continued His teaching and who authorized successors to do the same. (Scripture tells us that.) And it is that Church, the Church of Christ, that teaches us the beautiful truths about Mary.

And not only did Christ give us Mary, but Mary gave us Christ. This happens in three stages: past, present, and future.

First, it happened when she consented to be His Mother, at the Annunciation, when she said "Let it be to me according to your word" to God's angel, who asked her *permission* for the most important thing that ever happened, like a courteous gentleman. And *God deals with each of us in the same way He dealt with her.* The angel's word to her is also addressed to every one of the saved: "The Holy Spirit will come upon you, and the power of the Most High will overshadow you; therefore the child to be born will be called holy, the Son of God" (Lk 1:35). This is what happens to us too by faith and baptism when Christ is born in us, that is, when we are reborn in Him.

Second, she continues to do the same essential thing she did then, i.e., to say yes to Him, to will His will, which is our salvation. She does this by praying for our salvation and sanctification. How can Christ ignore the prayers of His own Mother? And how can her love and prayers be *less* passionate and powerful than any other human mother's love and prayers for her children? Think of these two facts together, and then you will see how powerful the Hail Mary is.

Third, she always will continue, both in time and in eternity, to show us what perfect Christlikeness means for a mere creature, for she is, as the poet says, "our tainted nature's solitary boast", the perfect saint.[3] She is that precisely because she is totally submitted to Christ. That is the essential meaning of a saint. Just as Christ is perfectly submitted to the Father (He is the perfect "surrenderer", the perfect "Muslim"), so is Mary to Christ. This totally unselfish other-directedness, this self-forgetful exaltation of the beloved other, is the essence of sanctity because it is the essence of ultimate reality, the eternal life of the Trinity. That is what scripture means when it says that "God *is* love" (1 Jn 4:8, emphasis added): that love "goes all the way up" to Heaven and the divine nature, as egotism and pride and hate and rivalry "go all the way down" to Hell and the character of the Devil.

So Mary is transparent with regard to Christ. That is why we are told so little about her in scripture: scripture is given to us on a "need-to-know" basis, and all we need to know about her, we see in Christ, since she is a finger pointing to Him. To quote a famous Zen saying about the proper use of words, "A finger is very useful for pointing at the moon, but the fool mistakes the finger for the moon." If we pay attention to her, we will not stop to sniff the pointing finger, like an ignorant animal, but will follow it to Christ. We will pray, "Show unto us the blessed fruit of thy womb, Jesus." And there is nothing she wants to do more than that. To use a crucial epistemological distinction from C. S. Lewis (in his essay "Meditation in a Toolshed"), if we are wise we will "look-along" rather than merely "look-at" this holy

---

[3] William Wordsworth, "The Virgin".

sign that always points to Christ. Among all the saints, she is our best icon.

In Catholic icons, Mary is seldom seen alone. Almost always she is seen with Christ, pointing to Christ, relative to Christ:

> in the Annunciation, when she conceives Christ;
> in the Nativity, when she gives birth to Christ;
> as the Madonna (Mother), surrounding and protecting the infant Christ;
> at the crucifixion, standing at His feet;
> in the Pietà, receiving His dead Body;
> in her Assumption *to Him* in Heaven;
> in her coronation *by Him* as "Queen of Heaven";
> surrounded with angels—*His* angels (2 Thess 1:7); and
> in her appearances on earth at Lourdes, Fatima, Loreto, or Guadalupe, to do *His* work.

We turn now to dogmas.

Protestants have no Biblical basis for objecting to the dogma of Mary's Assumption, for this happened to Enoch and Elijah too, according to scripture. It is merely an unscriptural assumption that it cannot happen to anyone else. *Her* Assumption is more scriptural than *their* assumption.

Her title as the "second Eve", which goes back to the earliest Church Fathers, is also Biblical. This is how the early Fathers interpreted Genesis 3:15, the "proto-Gospel". God arranged for a woman to have a real part in both the Fall and the Redemption—for God, unlike some Protestant theologians, is not a male chauvinist.

Mary's title as "Mother of God" historically was about Christ more than her: it guarded the doctrine of Christ's divinity against Arianism, as a mother guards her baby against its enemies, and as she and Joseph guarded Jesus against Satan's agent Herod by the holy family's flight into Egypt.

~

It is the dogma of Mary's Immaculate Conception that bothers Protestants the most, for this seems to make her the exception to the universal truth that all creatures need salvation. That is a strong argument, but there is a perfectly good answer to it. The dogma of her Immaculate Conception does *not* make Mary an exception to the universal truth that all men need salvation from sin. Christ saved Mary too, though in a different way. He saved others after they fell into sin; He saved her before she fell, by removing Original Sin from her at the moment of her conception, by sheer miracle and grace. We too are saved by sheer miracle and grace, but we first fall into the pit, then are hoisted out of it, while she is kept from falling into it—but both she and we are saved by the very same grace of the very same God. She was inoculated against the disease, while we were treated for it—by the very same divine Physician.

This dogma too is Christocentric. For the only reason Mary was made so uniquely "*full* of grace" (Lk 1:28, emphasis added) as to be immaculate is because she was to be made the Mother of God. She was made the perfect personal door for God to enter our world in person. Only the most perfect red carpet is appropriate for the greatest king to walk on. As the *Catechism of the Catholic Church* says, "*To become the mother of the Savior*, Mary 'was enriched by God with gifts appropriate to such a role.' "[4] What graces are appropriate to such a role? If we really know *that* role, i.e., if we really appreciate Christ, how can we limit our answer to that question? Would you minimize her to maximize Christ? Would you set them up as rivals? Would Christ have more glory if Mary had less? This would be not only to misunderstand Mary but to misunderstand Christ. Christ *shares* His grace and, by grace, His glory. That is why He came to earth! And that is the only reason we are saved: because He is not a miser.

Mary was as full of grace as a creature can be. She is triply united to the Triune God: the Father's perfect daughter, the Son's perfect Mother, and the Spirit's perfect spiritual spouse.

Not only is Mary no threat to the heart of Evangelicalism, but she is a tremendous aid to it. For the heart of Evangelicalism is Christocentrism, closeness to Christ, Christlikeness. If saintly Protestants like John Wesley or Hudson Taylor can aid an Evangelical toward that end, at least by their exemplary virtue, if not also by their intercessory prayers, would the Evangelical scorn their help? And why not by their continued prayers? Why should death lock an iron gate between the Church militant and the Church triumphant, so that they can no longer aid us by their prayers? Why would your physical mother stop loving you and praying for you now that she is in Heaven? And why would your spiritual Mother do that?

Protestants object to Catholic Mariology on the basis of

---

[4] *CCC* 490, emphasis added. The *Catechism* is quoting Vatican II, *Lumen Gentium*, 56.

their principle of Christocentrism, yet Mary was the single most Christocentric person who ever lived. What an irony! The real person and work and love of Mary—to bring us all, Protestants included, closer to Christ—totally contradicts the Protestant idea that the greatness and glory and grace in Mary are a dangerous idol that sucks Catholics' love and attention away from Christ.

But a person is stronger than an idea. Therefore, the real Mary will bring her protesting children home despite the idea-obstacles they erect.

The same priority of the real person over the abstract idea will "solve" other problems of ecumenism—e.g., how Christ is present in the Eucharist. The personal prayer I suggested in chapter 9 (see p. 54) will bring more Protestants home than any argument will because His Real Presence is more powerful than our ideas.

Mary will bring them home because she is a Mother, and "mother" is almost another word for "home".

29

Evangelism

Why do we need a "new evangelization"? Because the old one is failing.

Why is the old one failing? Why has the Catholic Church been steadily losing members to Protestant bodies, especially Pentecostal ones, especially throughout Latin America, and especially for the past century?

What is missing in the West? What was the secret of the Church's spectacular success in evangelizing the world in the first place? How did twelve confused Jewish boys convert the world? What did they have? What softened hard Roman hearts and hardened soft pagan heads?

Saints, of course.

But what produced so many saints?

Let's look at the history of saints. There were more canonized saints, as well as more martyrs, in the twentieth century than in all nineteen previous Christian centuries combined. That is, of course, because there were more people in the twentieth century than in all nineteen previous centuries. But the twentieth-century saints make up a much *smaller*, not larger, *percentage* of the population, at least in Western civilization, if not in the world at large.

Let's do some very simple math to see this.

How many Christians were there in the world in A.D. 100? Fewer than one hundred thousand, certainly. It was a very small percentage of a small world population. How many of them were saints or martyrs? Many. Many more than one thousand, certainly. This means that more than one in one hundred Christians was a saint or a martyr in A.D. 100. One percent. And that is probably a far too low estimate.

Now how many Christians are there in the world today? Over two billion. How many Christians would have to be saints and martyrs to equal the percentage in A.D. 100, which was one in one hundred? Twenty million! Are there twenty million saints and martyrs today? How many saints or martyrs are there? Let's say ten thousand. No, let's be generous and say twenty thousand. No, let's be very generous and say two hundred thousand. That's still only one-hundredth of twenty million.

So the early Church had, percentage-wise, one hundred times as many saints and martyrs. What was a normal expectation then is an exotic rarity now, even taking the world as a whole, where many Christians are martyred under anti-Christian totalitarian regimes; it is much much rarer here in the comfortable, decadent West.

Why? What gave them the courage to be martyrs, the joy to sing hymns as they were marched off to be eaten by lions, and the love to forgive their enemies as they were dying?

The answer is simple. The answer is Christ.

Christ was everything to them. He is not everything to us. He has to compete with consumerism and the sexual revolution and the internet and iPhones and BMWs and 401(k)s and HMOs and MTV—and He is not doing very well in the competition.

How many Christians today fully understand and appreciate and live Saint Paul's definition of life: "For to me to live is Christ, and to die is gain" (Phil 1:21)? (To die is gain because it is only more Christ.)

Why don't Catholics sing in church? It is not because they can't sing. They sing at parties and at ball games.

The answer is the same. The answer is Christ. When you know Christ, you can't *not* sing, even if your voice sounds like a crow. To know Him is to sing even in the Colosseum. If you hear a patient singing in the hospital, you know it is probably a Christian.

The question about singing is not superficial but fundamental. Singers converted the world. Everybody loves a singer, because singers are lovers, and everybody loves a lover.

To the early Christians, evangelism was not a task, and certainly not a "program". It was an inevitability: "We cannot but speak of what we have seen and heard" (Acts 4:20). It was like singing the praises of the one you're in love with. It *is*, precisely, singing the praises of the One you're in love with.

From the first, evangelism was "show and tell". Its argument was "Come and see" (Jn 1:39, 46). That was Christ's invitation to His first disciples—come and see *Me*—and that was His disciples' invitation to *their* disciples—come and see *Him*. When was that meant to stop? When was the Church meant to change from an organism to an organization?

What is true of evangelism is also true of catechesis, according to the *Catechism of the Catholic Church*. On evangelism, it says: "The transmission of the Christian faith [i.e., evangelism] consists primarily in proclaiming Jesus Christ."[1] And on catechesis, it says, "At the heart of catechesis we find, in essence, a *Person*" and that "in catechesis '*Christ* . . . is taught—everything else is taught with reference to him.' "[2]

But since the law of causality governs all things, you can't give what you don't have—you can't teach what you don't know. That is true both of intellectual knowledge and personal knowledge. *The* essential qualification for all Christian teachers, and the difference between success and failure, power and weakness, amazement and boredom, is this: Do you know Jesus Christ? Do you not just know *about* Him but *know* Him?

This is Jesus' prescription for winning the world. His last words to us on earth, Matthew 28:18–20, the "great commission", consists of just three propositions: a fact, a command, and a promise. The fact is "All authority in heaven and on earth has been given to me." The command is "Go therefore and make disciples of all nations, baptizing them . . . [and] teaching them." The promise is "Behold, I am with you always, to the close of the age." He *is* with us; the only question is, are we with Him?

"Jesus only" does not exclude Mary, or the Church, or dogmas, or sacraments, because all of these things are about Him. He comes to us with His Body the Church, and with His Mother, and in His sacraments. But it is indeed "Jesus only" (Mt 17:8) rather than "Jesus and" because *all* authority in Heaven and on earth has been given *to Him*. He has

[1] *CCC* 425.
[2] *CCC* 426, 427; emphasis added. The *Catechism* is quoting John Paul II, *Catechesi Tradendae*, 6.

authority over sin, because of His shed blood (Eph 1:7). He has authority over Satan, whom he saw fall like lightning from Heaven (Lk 10:18). He has authority over death because He conquered death and rose, and when we are incorporated into Him we are incorporated into His Resurrection (Rev 1:18). He has authority over Hell because its gates cannot prevail against His Church (Mt 16:18), which is us, the "people of God". He has authority over our fears because "perfect love casts out fear" (1 Jn 4:18), and He is infinite love. He sends us out into the world "as sheep in the midst of wolves" (Mt 10:16), and it is only the wolves who need to fear. He has authority over everything, from your piggy bank to your sex life, because He is the Lord, the one and only, and if we are going to live in the real world, we must live that central fact habitually, 24/7.

This "Evangelical evangelism" is not an alternative to "sacramentalism" but explains it and validates it. Because He speaks "as one who [has] authority, and not as their [the Jews'] scribes" (Mt 7:29), and because it is He who speaks when a Christian says, "I baptize you", baptism really saves us (1 Pet 3:21). (There it is in the Bible, as plain and simple as it can be. How can Biblical Protestants deny that? How could He put it more clearly?)

Evangelism is not an addition to the Gospel. It is a necessity of the Gospel. "Woe to me if I do not preach the Gospel!" (1 Cor 9:16). The Gospel is like the sun: it can't help shining. It is like God that way.

Evangelism is not merely an essential part of the Church's work but is also an essential part of the Church's food. It is how the Church grows. And she *must* grow. Her essence is to grow. If she doesn't grow, she dies, because she's alive.

She is an organism. She is not a memorial tombstone; she is a risen Body. She is not safe. She is Aslan.

If Catholics do not know the importance of evangelism as well as Protestants do, that tragedy is a key part of the division in the Body of Christ, because evangelizing is as much an essential aspect of the one true Church as teaching. We usually think that it is only because we cannot unite in dogma that we remain apart; but perhaps it is also because we cannot unite in evangelism.

~

The next question is: *How* do we evangelize? What do we say?

Do you want my answer or Jesus' answer?

Here is Jesus' answer: "When they bring you before the synagogues and the rulers and the authorities, do not be anxious about how or what you are to answer or what you are to say; for the Holy Spirit will teach you in that very hour what you ought to say. . . . I will give you a mouth and wisdom, which none of your adversaries will be able to withstand or contradict" (Lk 12:11–12; 21:15).

Most of us are not good speakers. Every year the polls show that our greatest fear is not death, or sin, or Hell, but public speaking! (This is not a joke. This is literally true.) And the more we fear something, the less competent we feel (and therefore the less competent we are) to talk about it. That is why it is easier for most parents to talk with their kids about soap or about Superman than about sex or about sanctity.

So how do we talk about Jesus? Jesus' simple answer to the "how" question is, as usual, Himself, His real presence, not just His example or His words in our memory. As usual, that real presence is the golden key that makes the difference between weakness and power.

What we say matters much less than what we are. "What you are speaks so loud I can hardly hear what you say." He wants us to be only His vocal cords, not His brains. If we rely on our own brains, our own thoughts and words, then our evangelism (or testifying, or proclaiming, or witnessing, or preaching, or sharing, or whatever we call it) will be either too slick or too clumsy, too arrogant or too apologetic, too pushy or too wimpy, too self-righteous or too sissified. But *His* evangelization is winsome and irresistible. So He tells us to rely on His mind and His Spirit, not ours. He is the Head; we just supply the body, the lungs, and the lips.

That doesn't mean that there is a guaranteed success. It doesn't mean that everyone we meet will instantly open the eyes of their hearts to the Light of the world. It is love, not magic. And love always appeals to free will. And free will means that even when the true light comes, people have the power to choose to shut their eyes and prefer comfortable darkness to uncomfortable light.

But even then they will know that there is something out there. When a really strong light shines, you can't help seeing something—a kind of red aura—even when you close your eyelids.

But what does this mean specifically, in practical terms? What are we to do? How are we to apply Jesus' directions? What is to be our methodology?

The very act of asking that question proves that we have misunderstood it. There is no methodology, no gimmick, no technology. Look again at what He says—and at what He doesn't say. The answer is in the text, and it couldn't be clearer. He gives us two commands, one negative and the other positive. The negative one is "Do not be anxious about . . . what you are to say", and the positive one is to simply believe and trust His promise that "the Holy Spirit will teach you in that very hour what you ought to say." That is all He says, and He adds nothing to it. We do. That is precisely our problem.

How can we not trust Him? He is God, not a con man; He doesn't lie. It's really, really simple. It's a "duh"! Our problem is that we're not simple enough to take Him at His word.

But how do we become simple and trusting and loving evangelists? At some point that question has to stop. "How?" means "With what technique?" But evangelism is love (it is our love-motivated matchmaking between the God of love and His beloved children), and love is not a technique. *The Art* [i.e., technique] *of Loving* is one of the stupidest titles ever invented. A technique is a way to make something easier—like lighting up a room by flipping a switch, or discovering facts by pressing buttons on a keyboard. But you can't make love any easier—essential love, i.e., *agape* love, the will to the good of the other—because, while in one sense love is the hardest thing in the world because it opposes our innate egotism, our original selfishness, yet it is also in a very real sense the simplest and easiest thing in the world: *you just do it*. That is all. It has no switch, no button, no formula, no cause. Everything else that ever happens, happens because something else causes it, but not love. Love can't be caused (made, made to exist, made to begin) by anything else at all except itself. For the cause can't be less than the effect, and everything else—*everything* else—is less than love. Love has no efficient cause because God is love and God has no efficient cause. That is why "Who made God?" is a really stupid question. It is exactly like the question "What causes love?"

God is love, and Christ is God incarnate; therefore, Christ is love incarnate. His "evangelism" is therefore merely

> Come and see, see Me, see for yourself, bump up against Reality, get to know Me, come closer, be really present, be honest, look at the *data*. Don't stop with ideas about Me—*come to Me*. For I come to you—I am coming to you at this very moment, and I will never, never stop coming to you. I will never stop short of the real you, the you that I designed from My eternity and for your eternity. I have come an infinite distance, from Heaven to earth, from eternity to time, from eternal life to this world of death. I came all the way down, into death and Hell itself ('My God, my God, why have you forsaken me?' [Mt 27:46]), just for this one purpose, for this meeting with you. And I have brought you an infinite distance for this meeting with Me, for I have brought you from nothing-ness to real being, by creating you. I am your Creator and designer. The secret of your identity is in Me, as the secret of Hamlet's identity is in Shakespeare. In coming to Me, you come to yourself.

Our "come and see" must be an extension of His "come and see". And because of the law of causality (again), because you can't give what you don't have, we can do this only if we are branches of that Vine. To show the Vine, you have to be the Vine. In other words, to win the world, we have to be saints. Just as the strongest argument against Christianity is Christians (bad Christians, joyless Christians, passionless

Christians), so the strongest argument for Christianity is Christians, i.e., saints. Saints are responsible for winning the world, and sinners are responsible for losing it.

This evangelizing by saints happened in the past, it is happening in the present, and it will happen in the future. The future will resemble the past. The world was snatched from Satan's jaws and won for Christ's love-feast when martyrs shed their bodies' blood and saints gave their souls' blood, like Christ, to win the world for Him. The world was snatched from Christ and won for Antichrist when tyrants and missionaries and inquisitors and pedophiles shed the blood of others' bodies or souls, like Dracula.

Evangelism is first of all not a matter of saying something, or even of doing something, but of being something: being Christ's Body, branches, fingers, lips. (Lips are for both kissing and speaking, showing and telling.)

Compare Saint Paul's success in Corinth with his failure in Athens. Compare 1 Corinthians 1–2 with Acts 17. In Athens Paul preached a marvelously beautiful and brilliant ecumenical sermon—and won two or three converts. In Corinth he "decided to know nothing among you except Jesus Christ" (1 Cor 2:2), and he won a city. There is no Pauline letter to the Athenians. There are two passionate and intimate letters to the Corinthians.

The essence of all real religion is total "surrender" (*islam*) to God—and God can use Muslims to remind us of that. The essence of Christianity, and the secret of evangelism, is our "islam" to Christ—and if Catholics have to go to Protestants to learn that, then let's go, immediately, for Christ's sake.

30

Ecumenism and World Religions

There are two reasons for including a chapter on world religions in a book on Protestantism and Catholicism even though this chapter will not say much about the differences between Protestants and Catholics on this issue. One reason is that there is a significant difference (though not a creedally defined difference) between typically Evangelical Protestant "exclusivism" and typically Catholic "inclusivism" here. The other reason is that the two problems of intra-Christian ecumenism and Christian–non-Christian comparative religions have parallel or analogous solutions.

Ecumenism

Unsurprisingly, the key to ecumenism is the same "golden key" that is the key to evangelism and, as we will see, to ecclesiology and to hermeneutics—Christ Himself, His real presence.

We can see this by looking at ecumenism's opposite, a kind of ecumenism of evil. For Christ unites His enemies as well as His friends. Pharisees and Sadducees, Romans and Jews, collaborators and rebels hated each other, but they hated

Him more. "Herod and Pilate became friends with each other that very day, for before this they had been at enmity with each other" (Lk 23:12).

C. S. Lewis wrote in the preface to *Mere Christianity*:

So far as I can judge from reviews and from the numerous letters written to me, the book, however faulty in other respects, did at least succeed in presenting an agreed, or common, or central, or "mere" Christianity. In that way it may possibly be of some help in silencing the view that, if we omit the disputed points, we shall have left only a vague and bloodless H.C.F. [highest common factor, British for lowest common denominator]. The H.C.F. turns out to be something not only positive but pungent; divided from all non-Christian beliefs by a chasm to which the worst divisions inside Christendom are not really comparable at all. If I have not directly helped the cause of reunion, I have perhaps made it clear why we ought to be reunited. Certainly I have met with little of the fabled *odium theologicum* from convinced members of communions different from my own. Hostility has come more from borderline people whether within the Church of England or without it: men not exactly obedient to any communion. This I find curiously consoling. It is at her centre, where her truest children dwell, that each communion is really closest to every other in spirit, if not in doctrine. And this suggests at the centre of each there is something, or a Someone, who against all divergencies of belief, all differences of temperament, all memories of mutual persecution, speaks with the same voice.[1]

---

[1] *Mere Christianity* (New York: Macmillan, 1943, 1960), 8–9.

Comparative Religions (Interfaith Dialogue)

Ecumenism in the proper sense of the word means ecumenical reconciliation and unity within Christianity, unifying the divided churches. Dialogue among world religions is not "ecumenical" dialogue but "interfaith" dialogue.

Interfaith dialogue is much harder than ecumenism because ecumenism has a common Christ as the common center. But there are parallels and analogies between ecumenism and interfaith dialogue, and some important common principles. Therefore, interfaith dialogue is relevant to Protestant-Catholic ecumenism. That justifies a brief look at it here.

In one sense the relation between Christianity and other world religions is obvious. There is good news and bad news. The good news is that there are massive agreements among all the religions of the world, especially in morality, and we must see them and use them. The bad news is that there are also real, substantive disagreements, real contradictions, especially in doctrine, in what is taught and believed. By far the most important of these contradictions is about Christ Himself. All Christians believe that He is God —if they don't, they are apostates, not Christians; and no non-Christians, whether religious or nonreligious, believe that He is God—if they did, they would be Christians.

Christ the Lord is the nonnegotiable center and essence of Christianity. So the only way a Christian can possibly conceive of unifying all the religions of the world is by the world's conversion to Christ. And the reason for that nonnegotiable conclusion is also nonnegotiable: the conversion of all the world to Christ is Christ's own clearly revealed will and command, in the "great commission" (Mt 28).

There is only one logically possible alternative to this "conservative" or "traditional" or "orthodox" position that sees the only solution to the problem of the relation between Christianity and all other religions as the whole world's conversion to Christ. The logic is simple and inescapable: since that traditional solution is obedience to Christ's own clearly revealed command, the only alternative is disobedience to that command, or else denial that Christ ever gave it, i.e., denial of our scriptural data. And that, in turn, necessarily presupposes that the Word of God, i.e., either Christ or scripture or both, is wrong. And that is not a form of Christianity; that is apostasy.

No matter how we rightly soften and nuance that, no matter what personal and pastoral and psychological additions we may rightly add to it, that is the objective, ontological core and unchangeable fact of the matter. *We* don't have to be hard and nonnegotiable, but Truth is.

This gives us an apparently unsolvable problem: if Christ is nonnegotiable, it seems that at the very heart and center, interfaith unity is impossible. And it seems even more impossible to claim that Christ, "a stone that will make men stumble, a rock that will make them fall" (1 Pet 2:8), could somehow be the key to positive relations with non-Christian religions, which deny His claim. And yet that is what I am going to suggest is true.

Jesus cannot be relativized. He cannot come under any more ultimate authority. He cannot be paralleled with Buddha or Muhammad or Moses. However, what He says about Moses might possibly be said about Buddha and Muhammad: that He comes to fulfill them and their laws, not to destroy them. Thus, Christianity could possibly include the essential positive claims of other world religions, as it claims to do with Judaism. But other religions could not include the essential positive claim of Christianity. Whatever generic unity there might be among world religions, it cannot be an essential one, because the very essence of one world religion, i.e., Christianity, is not generic but specific, distinctive, and offensive: that "Jesus Christ is Lord" (Phil 2:11; probably the very earliest Christian creed).

The way to true unity must always be truth, not compromise. Compromise is the way to a compromised unity; truth is the only way to true unity.

We looked at the inevitable and undeniable conclusion first. We can't deny that, but perhaps we can see something else if we look at the problem more carefully. Let's begin again at the logical beginning.

The "problem of comparative religions" is essentially that there are many different religions in the world, and they all seem to contradict each other at least on some essential things, especially in theology, although they also agree with each other on some equally essential things, especially in morality.

This is a very important problem for everyone because religion is and has always been the deepest and most passionate center and wellspring of the life of the human spirit, and therefore worldwide human unity depends largely on religious unity.

It is relatively easy for a weak Christian and a weak Muslim or Buddhist to be one with each other. A mild Red Sox fan and a mild Yankees fan can be friends and even enjoy a Red Sox–Yankees game together, because they both love the game itself more than they love their respective teams. But a passionate Red Sox fan and a passionate Yankees fan must be rivals to the end, at least in baseball, though not outside of it. A sign on the wall of a tunnel behind the stands in Fenway Park says, "Baseball is just a game. The Red Sox are serious."

Suppose someone proposed to these two fans that future games be played without keeping score, so that neither team would ever lose. After all, isn't it true that "it is better to travel hopefully than to arrive" and that process is more important than result? Of course, that is nonsense, but suppose they believed it? That would be not the consummation of baseball but its death. For the essence of the generic game is to determine a specific winner.

Now let's draw the analogy in comparative religions. Suppose someone proposed that we put away our differences and concentrate only on our universal agreements (e.g., by ignoring theology and focusing only on morality). That would be not the consummation of religion, either in general or in particular. That would be the death of religion. For religion is essentially particular. If a Christian ceased to believe that Christ is the unique Son of God and Savior, he would cease to be a Christian. If a Buddhist ceased to believe that Buddha was truly enlightened, that Nirvana was the ultimate truth, he would no longer be a Buddhist. If a Muslim came to believe that the Qur'an was not God's final and infallible revelation to mankind, he would not become a universalist Muslim or a completed Muslim or a modern Muslim but would cease to be a Muslim. If a Jew ceased to believe that Moses was God's prophet and that Mosaic law was God's law, he would cease to be a *religious* Jew. Each would abandon his religious absolute and substitute for it a vague, abstract lowest common denominator called "religion" in general.

So world religious unification seems in principle impossible.

Yet it actually happened once.

The whole world—at least the whole known world, the whole of Western premodern civilization, did embrace a single specific, particular, concrete religion (Christianity) once, for one thousand years.

How did that work? By conversion, of course. Not by interfaith dialogue.

Can what happened in the past in the West be a model and pattern for the same thing happening in the future throughout the whole world?

I honestly don't know the answer to that question. Almost everyone else, especially those who call themselves either "liberals" or "conservatives", seems to know the answer. The liberals "know" that the answer is no, and the conservatives equally "know" that the answer is yes.

How did the West move from many religions to one religion? Not by compromise but by conversion. That is simply a fact, whether this conversion was genuine and sincere or motivated by greed and gain and power and politics. It is a fact, whether the medieval form of religious unity was good, bad, or both. (All "liberals" say "bad"; most "conservatives" say "good"; I say "both".) The West attained religious unity by conversion. That is not controversial; that is fact. Does that sound naïve, simplistic, and unrealistic? But it is the only thing that ever did in fact work to unite the world, at least in the civilization we call the West.

Was that Christ's way? Yes. That too is not controversial;

that too is fact. Christ's solution to the "problem of comparative religions" is conversion to Him.

But—and this is the big "but"—that means not just the conversion of Hindus and Buddhists and Jews and Muslims to Christ but also, and first of all, the conversion of Christians to Christ.

The universal conversion won't happen until the particular conversion happens. The whole world will become Christian only when Christians become saints—and to the extent that Christians become saints.

That doesn't sound either "conservative" or "liberal". Or rather, it sounds both "conservative" and "liberal".

Universal conversion does not necessarily mean the condemnation of all non-Christians to damnation until they convert. In that sense it can be "inclusivistic" rather than "exclusivistic". Christ did not give His disciples comparative population statistics for Heaven and Hell, even when they asked for them (Lk 13:23). And this is not either a "liberal" point or a "conservative" point but is both, because the reason for this "liberal" hope for the salvation of non-Christians is the "conservative" dogma that Christ is not just a particular thirty-three-year-old, six-foot-tall Jew seen by only a few thousand Jews and later believed in explicitly by only a minority of the world's population in every century, but He is the eternal, universal *Logos*, the Word of God, the Mind of God "that enlightens *every* man" (Jn 1:9; emphasis added). As Saint Justin Martyr said in the second century, if Socrates said yes to this *Logos*, and lived and died for it, he was a Christian even though he never heard about Christ and even if he was confused about whether this *Logos* was an "It" or a "He".

The "scandal of particularity", the "narrow way" doctrine ("I am the way. . . . No one comes to the Father, but by me" [Jn 14:6]), was taught not by a mere man but by the *Logos*, the eternal, universal mind of the one God of all men who became this one man. Since He is the one who enlightens every man, whatever light non-Christians have, they have from Christ. That is the "conservative" way of stating the truth, the very same truth as the "liberal" truth that God loves all men and wills to save even non-Christians. This "liberal" hope is based on the fact that Christ is already present in all the light, all the truth, present in all the religions of the world. He is *hiddenly* present, but He is *really* present. Therefore, all the truth in all the religions can be and should be and must be and will be preserved, not forgotten, in the future worldwide growth of Christianity. (Yes, Christianity grows. It is alive.) All truth is His truth, He who said not "I teach the truth" but "I *am* . . . the truth" (Jn 14:6; emphasis added).

If all light is from the one Christ, it follows that insofar as non-Christian religions fully follow their light, they must eventually meet and come together with each other and with Christianity, since all light comes from the same single source. For "everything that rises must converge", as Flannery O'Connor said, quoting Teilhard de Chardin. (Teilhard's was a mind with both many confusions *and* many illuminations.)

We are at present far from knowing what form such a recognition of Christ in other religions might take, or even whether it will happen at all. But we do know that the only possible basis for unity is truth, and if Christ is who He says He is ("I *am* the truth"), then He is the one key to all true unity. And if He is not who He says He is, then He is not one of many great religious wise men at all but either the most arrogant blasphemer and liar who ever lived, if He knew He was only a man when He claimed to be God, or else an insane lunatic, if He was not God but believed He was. For the gap between what you are and what you believe you are is a measure of your insanity, and there is no greater gap than the gap between the finite creature and the infinite Creator God.

Christ's claim constitutes the single major "problem of comparative religions". It is unique. No other wise man ever claimed to be the one God and Savior. This claim seems to be the greatest obstacle to religious unity. All Muslims say to Christians, "We revere your prophet; why do you not revere ours?" All Hindus say to Christians, "We revere your yoga; why do you not revere ours?" (Hindus see all religions as yogas, or different ways to practice the same discipline to lead or bind us to God, many roads up the same mountain.) How can this Christian "scandal of particularity" possibly be the key to universality and unity? How can Christ be the key that opens the door to world religious unity? His claim seems definitively to close it.

The Christian claim about Christ sounds egotistic, narrow-minded, and arrogant to non-Christians. Christians reply that their claim is not egotistic because it is not their claim but His; that it is not narrow-minded because it is the only ground for universal unity; and that it is not arrogant but humble because we Christians dare not arrogate to ourselves the authority to change it, to correct our Lord's words, to edit God's mail rather than delivering it intact. We have no such authority because we are not the authors of it. If we are the authors of it, then it is indeed the world's most egotistic, narrow-minded, arrogant, and blasphemous lie. Christianity can't possibly be just one of many good religions: it is either the best or the worst, the ultimate truth or the ultimate lie. Like Christ Himself.

The "scandal of particularity" is not a dispensable addition to Christianity. We can, however, soften the scandal a bit by explaining how this apparently unreasonable "one way to Heaven" doctrine is really quite reasonable.

The most common image used against the "exclusivism" of Christianity is the image of "many roads up the same mountain". All men seek God; how dare anyone say his road to God is the only one? This argument makes sense if the image is accurate, and the image is accurate if and only if all these roads are made by us, as roads from the bottom of the mountain to the top, i.e., if all religion is man's search for God. But what if Christianity is God's search for man? What if Christ is God's search for man? What if Christ is the one way up because He is the one way down? What if Christ is not divinized man but humanized God? What if this one road is the road down the mountain, i.e., a road God made, not man? How could man's roads, however good or true or beautiful, possibly be equal to God's road?

All other religions teach that the way to God is some doctrine or enlightenment or practice taught by some man, some God-inspired or God-seeking prophet, saint, or mystic; that the way to God is to obey a God-given law (Judaism, Islam) or to transform human consciousness (Hinduism, Buddhism) or to be good enough or sincere enough or nice enough (modern Western humanism). Only Christianity says that the way is a Person. All other religions say,

"This is the best way up"; Christ says, "I am the one way down."

Christians do not deny that this divine Person manifests different aspects of Himself in many different ways in many different religions—for scripture says that God has revealed Himself "in many and various ways" (Heb 1:1), and these ways are probably much more numerous and diverse than we can dream. But this same scripture goes on to say that now "he has spoken to us by a Son" (Heb 1:2), who is the full revelation of the Father (Col 1).

If Christ is who He claims to be, then Muhammad cannot be His equal precisely because of the essential truth of Muhammad's Islam, that there is "no God but God". It is precisely because of this absolute truth of Islam, not in denial of it, that Christians accept the absolute truth of Christianity. Christians are Christians only because they are good Muslims, good "surrenderers" to the one God.

There is a pattern here for all conversions to Christianity. We have data on this from Christ Himself, who said that good Jews become good Christians not despite the fact that they are good Jews but because of it—not just because they are good people but because they are good Jews. And when Jews become Christians now, they almost always say that they are now completed Jews, more Jewish than non-Christian Jews are, not less. They become Christians by being faithful to their own Judaism, their own prophets. For Christ says, "Do not think that I have come to abolish the law and the prophets; I have come not to abolish them but to fulfil them" (Mt 5:17).

Judaism is unique because it is the first part of the one divinely revealed road down the mountain rather than one of the many man-made roads up. Nevertheless, we can see a pattern here holding true for all non-Christian religions. Take paganism, which is as different from Judaism as you can get. Even there, we find Christ anonymously present. Missionaries to pagan lands are typically amazed at the Christian clues, hints, or guesses they find in pagan religions: dying and rising savior gods, stories of the Creation and the Fall, promises of redemption, and a worldwide knowledge of the one supreme Spirit who is all-good, all-powerful, and all-knowing, however hidden this wisdom is behind later layers of superstition, polytheism, and pragmatism.

Might there not be indeed, as Raimundo Pannikar claims, an "unknown Christ of Hinduism"? Might not the Tao of Taoism be, as Hiermonk Damascene claims in his book *Christ the Eternal Tao*, another word for the *Logos*? Might not Buddhist transformation of consciousness be ontologically not wholly different from Jesus' "new birth", as Dom Aelred Graham suggests in *Zen Catholicism*?

My honest answer to these questions is: I don't know. Most "liberals" claim to know that the answer is yes, and most "conservatives" claim to know that the answer is no, but I don't know. I take my clues from Pope Saint John Paul the Great, who was both a totally orthodox and traditional Christian and the most boldly ecumenical pope who ever lived. He was both of these things (the typically "conservative" thing and the typically "liberal" thing) for the very same ultimate reason: his Christocentrism.

And that Christocentrism is the common point of both traditional Protestant Evangelicalism and of the new *Catechism of the Catholic Church* and of the Catholic "new evangelization".

The Universality of Christ

Let's begin again from the most scandalously "exclusive" point in our Christian data: "Jesus said to him, 'I am the way, and the truth, and the life; no man comes to the Father, but by me'" (Jn 14:5–6).

The way, the truth, and the life are the three things we all need the most and therefore desire the most, deep down. "The way" is goodness; "the truth" is truth; and "the life" is spiritual life, beauty, bliss, and joy. Goodness, truth, and beauty are the three essential foods of the soul.

They are also the objects of the soul's three distinctively human powers (the will, the mind, and the heart). Plato called these three powers of the soul the "spirited part", the "reason", and the "appetites". Freud called them, in a very reduced form, the ego, the superego, and the id.

They correspond to the three dimensions in every religion: code, creed, and cult; or works, words, and worship. They are dimensions of a single reality, like the three dimensions of space. It is the very same reality that Christians obey in their morality, confess in their theology, and participate in in their liturgy. That "very same reality" is Christ. These three *dimensions* are not three *parts*; you can separate parts in reality as well as in thought; you can separate dimensions only in thought.

By the way, the three Persons of the Trinity are neither three dimensions nor three parts. Nor are they three beings, or three substances (entities). They are one being, one substance, in three Persons.

"The way, the truth, and the life" parallel the three likenesses to God in the human soul. "The way" is Godlikeness in our will and our moral life: holiness, sanctity, *agape* love. "The truth" is Godlikeness in our mind: wisdom, light, true enlightenment. "The life" is Godlikeness in our feelings, emotions, desires, creativity, imagination, and intuition. This category is more slippery and difficult to define than the other two. Perhaps our culture has not yet achieved clarity about it, as Plato's threefold division of the soul had not yet achieved clarity about the will, which he called simply the "spirited part".

Saint John's terms for these three Godlike qualities, especially in his first Epistle, are love, light, and life. All three reflect the whole God, but within the Trinitarian Godhead they correspond primarily to (1) the Father, whose will is the supreme good; (2) the Son, who is the *Logos*, the light, and the Word, the Mind of God; and (3) the Spirit, who is the beatitude and joy of the love between Father and Son, as beauty is the child of the marriage of goodness and truth.

Hinduism identifies these three things as *sat-chit-ananda* —*sat* and *chit* and *ananda*, the three knowable attributes of Brahman, the supreme God: infinite being, infinite understanding, and infinite joy; the supreme good, the supreme wisdom, and the supreme beauty.

The pattern is universal. And Christ is its fulfillment. He brings the whole Godhead to mankind. Whenever any will chooses good, it chooses Him, because He *is* the way. Whenever any mind knows truth, it knows Him, because He *is* the truth. Whenever any heart loves life and beauty, it enjoys Him, for He *is* the life. It was Christ who motivated the goodwill and good deeds of Pericles, and who enlightened the mind of Socrates, and who inspired the plays of Sophocles, even though they did not know it. For all goodness is His goodness, all truth is His truth, all beauty is His beauty.

If we deny that, if we deny that everyone, even non-Christians, can touch Him, then we deny that *He* touches *them*. If we deny them access to Him, we deny Him access to them. And then we reduce him to a tribal god, a finite part of the whole greater picture that we call "comparative religions". Ronald Knox called such "comparative religion" "the best way to make a man comparatively religious". If the pious agnostic Socrates did not die for the true God, if he did not love Christ in loving the "unknown god", then there must be other lovable gods than Christ.

Thus, this scandalous "one way" doctrine of John 14:6 is inclusive, not exclusive. Christ is not confined to Christianity; He moves also beyond it. But Christianity is confined to Christ; it does not move beyond Him. There is more to Christ than Christianity, but there is no more to Christianity than Christ.

Protestants who make this "inclusive" point are usually liberals, and Protestants who make this "exclusive" point usually tend to fundamentalism. Catholics transcend both because they have a stronger and older tradition of connecting them: e.g., the works of Saint Justin Martyr, Saint Clement of Alexandria, Saint Thomas Aquinas, and Saint John Paul II (see *Dominus Iesus*).

The Distinctiveness of Christianity

If Christ is active also outside Christianity, then why be a Christian rather than anything else? If there is no answer to that question, there is no compelling reason to be a Christian. We choose our cars and computers and cameras because we believe one brand is superior to others. No one advertises, "Our product is no better than any other.

They're all the same." If you don't believe that your religion is superior to all others, there is no reason to buy it, to believe it, to practice it.

How is Christianity distinctive and better? What did Christ give to the world that no one else did? The answer is stunningly simple: He gave the world God.

Imagine a world bazaar of religions. (I know the idea of such a bazaar is bizarre.) What does each offer you?

The religious Jew will offer you the Torah, the Mosaic law.

The Muslim will offer you the Qur'an.

The Hindu will offer you various yogas, techniques for transforming your consciousness and attaining mystical experience.

The Buddhist will offer you the Four Noble Truths and the Noble Eightfold Path to Nirvana.

The Taoist will offer you the *Tao te ching*: simple advice about the Way of ultimate reality, of nature, and of wisdom, and how to live it.

The Confucian will offer you elaborate prescriptions for harmony in family, state, and society, in the *Analects*.

The Christian will offer you Jesus Christ, God incarnate.

Even if Moses' law is God's law, God's law is not God. Christ gives you God.

Even if the whole Qur'an is God's whole word (which it can't be because it denies Christ's claim), God's written word is not God. Christ gives you God.

Even if Hindu yoga gives you a more Godlike consciousness (which I think it can't because consciousness is not yet love, and God is love), consciousness is not God. Christ gives you God.

Even if Buddhism or Taoism or Confucianism gives you

the deepest philosophical truth about yourself (which it can't because neither Buddha nor Lao Tzu nor Confucius designed and created you), truth about yourself is not even truth about God, much less God Himself. Christ gives you God.

All other religious teachers—except egomaniacs, fakers, tyrants, and money-mad manipulators—subordinated themselves to their message.

Moses and Muhammad claimed to be prophets of God. Christ was not satisfied with being called a prophet of God (see Mt 16:13–19) because He was the one who sent the prophets.

Buddha said, "Look not to me; look to my *dharma* (doctrine)." Christ said, "Come to me" (Mt 11:28). Buddha said, "Be lamps unto yourselves." Christ said, "I am the light of the world" (Jn 9:5).

Any other religion could survive without its founder. If Abraham or Moses or Muhammad or Buddha or Confucius or Lao Tzu turned out to be mythical figures and not real historical people at all, the religions that they founded would still survive, just as Shakespeare's plays would still retain their power and appeal if it were discovered that Shakespeare never existed, that the name was a pseudonym for Marlowe or De Vere or Bacon or even Queen Elizabeth. But Christianity cannot survive without Christ, without a real, present, live, resurrected Christ. Because you can't be saved by a dead Savior.

All religious founders claim to teach the way. Christ alone claims to *be* the way. All religious founders claim to teach the truth. Christ alone claims to *be* the truth. All religious founders claim to teach a higher life. Christ alone claims to *be* the life.

But this is not anti-ecumenical and disunifying, as it seems to be at first. Rather, this is supremely ecumenical and unifying. For Christ is the way and the truth and the life that all religions teach. Insofar as they teach goodness, truth, and beauty, they teach Christ.

Thus, religious universalism, or inclusivism, and Christian particularism, or exclusivism, are not mutually contradictory but mutually complementary.

This sounds paradoxical, but it is logical:

Premise 1: All religious founders claim to teach the way, and the truth, and the life.

Premise 2: Christ claims to be the way, the truth, and the life.

Conclusion: Insofar as the claims of other religions are true, it logically follows that all other religions teach something about Christ.

So whatever particular truths are in all the world's religions, are present and fulfilled in the truth of the unique claim of Christ. The truths of world universalism are compatible with and fulfilled in the truth of Christian particularism. All their true words are in *the* Word. The answer to the "scandal of particularity" by an "inclusivism" of all religions is logically compatible with and is fulfilled in the "exclusivism" of the Christian "scandal of particularity" itself.

But even if all religions are true, even profoundly true, this does not mean that all religions are *totally* true (free from error) or *equally* true. For only one religion centers on the only sane man who ever claimed to *be* the truth.

And the connection between this point about comparative religions and the point about Protestant-Catholic ecumenism is this: as Christ fulfills all the truths in other religions, Catholicism fulfills all the truths in Protestant "mere Christianity".

I showed this in the long last chapter in my *Handbook of Catholic Apologetics.*[2]

[2] Peter J. Kreeft and Ronald K. Tacelli, *Handbook of Catholic Apologetics: Reasoned Answers to Questions of Faith* (San Francisco: Ignatius Press, 2009), 443–46.

31

The Church

What is the Church? In one sense that is the fundamental issue dividing Catholics and Protestants. All the things Catholics believe that Protestants don't believe are things Catholics believe because the Church teaches them, even if they're not explicitly present in the Bible (at least to Protestant eyes). Logically, *sola scriptura* is the fundamental Protestant premise that justifies all the distinctively Protestant and non-Catholic positions.

So to understand the divide, we must understand the nature of the Church.

The stock contrast today in Western culture is between Jesus and the Church, or "organized religion". "I'm not religious, but I'm spiritual" is fast becoming the West's most popular religion. Almost no one bad-mouths Jesus, but nearly everybody bad-mouths "organized religion".

But if we look at what Jesus Himself said about organized religion, we find that the critique of it as un-Christian is simply self-contradictory. For Jesus gave us organized religion, i.e., a Church.

By the way, those inside this organized religion never speak of organized religion. It is more like disorganized religion. Was Noah's ark organized? Yes, in its beginning, by divine command: such a kind of wood, and such and such dimensions, and animal species two by two. But in its life? Did Noah's sons think they were in "organized religion" when they shoveled all that animal poop? And that is what the Church, and everything human, is full of. The Church, like man, is human in her life, though she is divinely created. In God's world, "everybody poops", even popes.

~

There are three ways of looking at the Church. Only one of them lets you love her.

To many people, the Church looks like an organization, one that is old, big, clumsy, obtuse, irrelevant, and oppressive. She is predictably human and fallible yet, unpredictably, claims to be divine and infallible. That is what she looks like, that is the "Church visible", to unbelievers. She is not lovable, even though many of her saints and songs, her bells and whistles, may be.

To a second group of people, the Church is an ethereal, spiritual, mystical thing, the "Church invisible", an ideal in the mind of God, a set of perfect principles or ideals, whether a liberal "political correctness" or a traditionalist ossification and idealization of the best of the past. That is not lovable either because only a concretely real being is lovable, not an idea or an ideal.

The third, and only true, way of looking at the Church is Joan of Arc's way. When Joan's judges tried to confuse her about the issue, she replied, "About Jesus Christ and the Church, I simply know they're just one thing, and we shouldn't complicate the matter."

When she said that the Church and Christ, Body and Head, are one thing, Joan was not saying that the Church was simply perfect. For she said that to the wicked bishops who were plotting to kill her! Nor was Joan a fundamentalist or a Gnostic or a "spiritualist" who set up "me and Jesus alone" against "organized religion", even though she had private mystical experiences.

What the Church understands by the Church is what Joan of Arc understood: the Church is, most fundamentally, the Body of Christ. And your body is you. Christ is the "Head" of this Body, not as Bill Gates was the head of Microsoft but as that round, hairy ball between your shoulders is the head of your body. Christ is the Head of a living Body; a corpus, not a corpse; an organism, not an organization; a real, concrete Body, not a legal fiction or an abstract ideal. A body is not less concrete than its head.

That is why Christ says, "As you did it to one of the least of these my brethren, you did it to me" (Mt 25:40)— because He is the vine and we are the branches (Jn 15:5) of one and the same living organism (which is both spiritual and physical, like ourselves and like Christ Himself). The *word* "vine" that Christ used is a metaphor, of course, since the Church is not a literal biological vine; but the Church is just as literal and real and concrete and particular and physical as a grapevine. And the oneness of Christ and His people is just as literally real as the oneness of a grapevine and its branches. Both "vines" live by a single life. The single life, the single blood, of the Church is Christ's blood.

Unlike earthly vines, this vine has its roots in Heaven and its foliage on earth. It is an upside-down vine. The Church is the "extension of the Incarnation". That is why she must be visible. She is a sacrament, like Christ, who is the primary sacrament.

She is as concrete as Christ is, both in the sense of being an actual individual entity and in the sense of being material. This materiality shocks our expectation that "religion" should be something "spiritual". But it is Biblical. The woman who touched the hem of Jesus' garment was healed; those who touched others' garments were not, even if their souls were holier. Those who eat the consecrated communion wafer eat God; those who eat other bread do not, even if their souls are holier. The literal blood that literally poured from His literal Body on the Cross literally saved us; no other blood could do that.

For it is not true that all you need is good intentions. You also need objective reality. It is not true that "all you need is love." You need Christ's love. Your own is not enough.

Christ does not save us without His Body. Without His bodily death and bodily Resurrection, we have no hope (see 1 Cor 15). We may not understand why that is so, we may not understand the spiritual technology of salvation, but it is very clear from the New Testament that that is so. "The flesh is the hinge of salvation", says the ancient Church Father Tertullian.

It is a syllogism.

> Premise 1: Without the Body of Christ, there is no salvation.
>
> Premise 2: The Church is the Body of Christ.
>
> Conclusion: Without the Church, there is no salvation.

From the beginning, Jesus' Church has always taught this principle, that outside the Church there is no salvation (*extra ecclesiam nulla salus*). It is implied in Matthew 18:17–18, Ephesians 1:22–23, Colossians 1:17–19, and 1 Timothy 3:15.

But the Church also teaches that this does not mean that all *who do not know* that the Church is Christ's Body and who therefore remain outside her are damned. It means that all who are saved, whoever they are and however many or few they are, are saved through the Church, whether they know it or not. It is with the Church exactly as it is with Christ: He is the only Savior (He says so Himself!), but that does not mean that those who know this are the only ones who are saved. It means that all who are saved, whether they call themselves Christians or not, are saved by Him. Exactly the same principle applies to the Church, because Head and Body are inseparable. All who are saved are saved by His Church, whether they know it or not. For the Church cannot be decapitated. Nor can Christ be deprived of His Body.

~

Next point: this Church can be identified. She has "marks". Four of them are that she is (1) one, (2) holy, (3) universal ("catholic"), and (4) apostolic. (That is from the Nicene Creed, which is accepted by Protestants as well as Catholics.)

Protestant churches are not one but many: there are over twenty thousand of them.

Protestants are often holy, but they do not claim that their churches are.

Protestant churches are partial, not universal.

And Protestant churches do not even *claim* material apostolic succession, through the visible sacrament of holy orders.

If Christ's true Church were not visible, how could we identify her? We need to identify her visibly and publicly because we need to find her objective reality. Our own personal, private, human, subjective, spiritual goodwill and intelligence are not enough. Is that enough for your surgeon, your financial adviser, or your pilot? We need honest intentions, of course, but we also need objective reality—especially when we are dealing with something divine.

Suppose the Church were not divine but only human. Suppose she were our invention. Suppose the Church, unlike Christ, had only one nature, not two: that she were only human, not divine, as "modernist" or "liberal" or "humanist" theology claims about Christ. In that case we ourselves would have to figure out the right understanding of scripture, without divine authority. We would have to discover the truth about the Trinity, and the two natures of Christ, and baptism, and the Eucharist, and saints, and Mary, and Purgatory, and the Church herself, and crucial and controversial moral issues like abortion and marriage and homosexuality and euthanasia and contraception and war and capital punishment and money. Under this supposition, who could ever know with certainty the will of God? And how could the Church ever be one? There would be twenty thousand different churches, each teaching its own sincere but fallible human opinion.

In other words, Protestantism.

The Church is our only link to Christ. Without the Church, Christ is two thousand years distant in time and thousands of miles distant in space. What bridges the space-time gap to make us "contemporaneous with Christ"? What brings Christ to me across the millennia and the miles? The Church does that, did that from the beginning, and will do that until the end of the world.

The only other answer to that question is the Holy Spirit.

That is true, that is necessary—but not sufficient. For the Holy Spirit, unlike the Church, is not visible. Every heretic, fanatic, and inventor of a new religion in history believed he was inspired by the Holy Spirit, just as every heretic in history has appealed to the Bible.

After Christ ascended into Heaven, every Christian who ever learned of Christ and converted to Christ did so through the ministry of the Church. From the earliest apostolic times, to become a Christian was not merely to change your beliefs; it was, essentially, to accept baptism into the Church. It was like getting married, or joining the army. It was as visible and concrete and identifiable as walking through a door. It was not just a change of personal, private beliefs. That is a historical fact, not a sectarian Roman Catholic dogma.

We know Christ today only because the Church has brought Him to us, both by word and by sacrament. "Word" means "witnessing", preaching, missioning—and writing and canonizing the Bible. The New Testament is part of that witness. It was the Church that wrote it, preached it, and later defined it (i.e., canonized it, told us what books were rightly included in it). That too is a historical fact, not a sectarian dogma. Without the authority of the Church, how can we know that the Gospel of John is divine revelation and the Gospel of Thomas is not? Martin Luther sincerely disagreed with the Church when the Church told him that the Epistle of James was part of the Bible, because James explicitly contradicted Luther's central belief that we are justified by faith alone (Jas 2:24). Try to contradict the essence of Protestantism more simply, absolutely, clearly, and literally than James 2:24 does; it can't be done. God could just as well have written: "Protestantism's primary principle, justification by faith alone, is not true" as the next verse, if He had been into historical anachronisms.

~

If your Protestant principle is "Jesus only", I will prove the Catholic conclusion from your own premise. If you believe in Jesus only, you must believe in Jesus completely. So you must look at everything He said. And therefore, you must accept the Church *because He told you to*.

Also, please remember the simple fact that you learned to believe in Christ in the first place only because the Church told you to. If you say, "No, it was my parents and teachers who told me", I reply that they did that as part of the Church, the chain of witnesses to Christ that began two thousand years ago. They didn't make it up out of their own minds! They learned it. From whom? Other teachers. There is a chain stretching back to Christ. We believe in Him only because we trust that chain. That chain is the Church. If the Church is not trustable, if the Church is only human and fallible, then what we know of Christ is not trustable but only human and fallible. The chain is broken.

The Church points us to Christ. That is her whole business in this world. And Christ points us to the Church. Read the New Testament and you will see this very clearly.

For a thousand years the Church was only one: one visible Church for all mankind. The Church expressed this truth by calling herself the "Catholic" Church. "Catholic" means "universal". That too is a historical fact, not a sectarian dogma.

The Church is Christ's Body, and He has only one Body. He is not a monster. The Body is also His bride, and He is not a polygamist.

~

The Body of Christ is one and the same Body in four places.

1. It is His universal Body the Church, both visible and invisible, as human nature is both visible and invisible. When we enter the Church by baptism, we are "incorporated", i.e., literally "in-bodied", into Him.

2. It is His personal Body and Blood that He gave us on the Cross for our salvation.

3. It is that same Body and Blood that He gives us in the Eucharist.

4. It is the Body that ascended into Heaven and is our eternal home.

The Church has uniformly taught these four things from the beginning. That too is not a sectarian dogma but a historical fact. Not a single Christian denied the Real Presence of Christ in the Eucharist for one thousand years (in fact, with a very few heretical exceptions, for fifteen hundred years).

We receive Him today not just by thinking about Him but by eating Him. You are what you eat. We become the "Body of Christ" (the Church) by eating the "Body of Christ" (the Eucharist). If this is not true, Catholics are cannibals and idolaters. How could the Holy Spirit have allowed such a universal atrocity for fifteen hundred years, especially after Christ promised His Church that He would lead them into all truth (Jn 16:13) and be with them until the end of the world (Mt 28:20)?

~

But the Church's priests abused innocent little boys, and her bishops covered it up. Five hundred years ago even some of her popes were the religious equivalent of the Mafia. Most of her members look more like Ned Flanders than Jesus Christ. Like a wise but witchy old lady, the Church often seems bitchy, manipulative, fearful, cantankerous, sour, melancholy, platitudinous, and paranoid. Worse, she has often been unfaithful. God often calls His chosen one, Israel, a whore in the Old Testament, and He calls two of the seven churches in Asia similarly insulting names in Revelation. And it is quite clear what Jesus would say about the recent priest sex scandals: it was something about millstones (Mt 18:6; Mk 9:42; Lk 17:2). God commanded Hosea to marry a whore because He wanted to show us who we were. Beauty fell in love with a beast. It's easy, or it ought to be easy, for us to fall in love with God, with Beauty; but it seems impossible for Beauty to fall in love with a beast. But that's the impossible Good News. He told us not to cast our pearls before swine (Mt 7:6), but He did that very thing.

~

In light of this last point, how can we still say that the Church and Christ are "just one thing", as Joan of Arc did? The simple answer is that we say that because Christ Himself said it: "I am the vine, you are the branches" (Jn 15:5). A vine and its branches are not two things. The life of the vine and the life of the branches are not two things. The branches do not imitate the vine—they live on the very lifeblood or sap of the vine. Imitation is "monkey business". When monkeys imitate human activities, they do not become human, just ridiculous.

Let's go deeper into that fundamental point, the identity of the Church as Christ's own Body (visible *and* invisible). My goal here will be not to refute Protestants but to "Catholicize" their notion of the Church.

If we are His Body, His branches, His "members" (i.e., organs!), then we do not merely adore and obey and love Him; we live in Him. There is only one sap in vine and branches, only one blood in Head and Body, one life in Christ and Christian. The New Testament word for that life is not *bios* (natural life, human life) but *zoe* (supernatural life, divine life).

If you say this sounds too pantheistic, I reply simply that Christ Himself said it. If He didn't mean it, why did He say it?

If our union with Christ—the *Church's* union with Christ, for the Church is the "*people* of God" as well as the "Body of Christ"—is not that total, that intimate, that "mystical", that almost-pantheistic; if we are not "in" Christ as literally as a branch is in a vine; if that is only an exaggeration or a metaphor, then the deepest desire of all lovers is never attained and is forever frustrated when it comes to His love for us. For lovers desire union above all things. They desire not to be free from each other but to be bound to each other. They desire to be free only from whatever keeps them from being bound. When lovers wax mystical, they say things like, "Love you? I *am* you."

It is conceivable that any human love may be forever

frustrated, but it is not conceivable that God's love is. The force that effects this union is not our love for Him but His love for us. All we do is choose to allow it to happen. But that free choice is necessary too, not just because of us but because of God; not just because we have free will but also, and ultimately, because God is a gentleman and will not come uninvited. He will not impose Himself; He will not rape our souls. But He will have us, He will *be* us, as Christ *is* man as well as God. The perfect God will have the perfect union that perfect love demands. He will unite Himself to us, and us to Him, as totally and as intimately as is metaphysically possible. And He will not rest until that is accomplished. (That is the fundamental reason why there is a Purgatory.)

This divine union is not isolated and individualistic. That is angelism. We are not angels. We are family.

The bodily union with Christ is not sexual, but sex is an icon of it, a holy picture of it. That is why sex is holy. (It is all in John Paul II's "theology of the body". Look it up. Everyone who does comes back "sold".)

Only because the Church's union with Christ is as total as the union of the branches with the vine does He say to her that "apart from me you can do nothing" (Jn 15:5). If we were merely imitators, apprentices, disciples, or students of Christ, we could do something on our own. The student can learn a bit on his own without the teacher, but the branch cannot have any life on its own apart from the vine.

Many Christians—Calvinists especially, who are in many ways the Christian equivalent of non-Sufi Muslims—tend to be deeply suspicious of that mystical union because they think it sails too close to the rocks of pantheism and imperils the infinite distinction between divine Creator and human creature. But God Himself overcame that distinction, in the Incarnation! Far from threatening the divine sovereignty (the fundamental insight of Calvinism), the mystical union expresses it and fulfills it, for at least three reasons: (1) It is the will of the sovereign God. (2) It is accomplished only by the grace of God ("Everything is grace", said Saint Thérèse). (3) On our part the relationship is one of total dependency on God, unlike the student-teacher relationship or the imitation relationship. It is total "surrender" (*islam*). Like love. No, it is not *like* love; it *is* love. His love is not like ours; ours is like His. As we said, *agape* love is not like sex; sex is like it. *That* is why sex is so ecstatic.

When we let Christ's words sink into our hearts, we find that He is not safe and soothing but shocking and bracing like a sudden shower of ice in summer or a blast of fire in winter. The experience is always far more than we expected. To actually live in Him as a branch lives in the vine—this is not something "mystical" in the popular, misunderstood sense of something vague, sweet, and dreamy. That kind of "myst-i-cism" begins in mist, centers in I, and ends in schism. No, this is as concrete and shocking as "You must eat my flesh and drink my blood" (cf. Jn 6:53–54).

In fact, it is not *like* that; it *is* that. We become the Body of Christ by eating the Body of Christ. For Christ's real presence in the Eucharist is not just the presence of the gardener to the branches but the presence of the vine to the branches. It is not just the presence of the love of the philanthropist but the presence of the love of the Husband. The two become one. It is more intimate, not less, than we can imagine.

It is from this perspective alone that we can rightly under-

stand the Church's claims to her authority and our obedience. (Yes, "her" authority—the Church is a "she", because He is a "he". That is His language, and that of all
the great saints and mystics. If you don't like it, that means
there is something wrong with you, not with Him.) The
basis for the Church's authority is not legal and forensic
but metaphysical and mystical. Christ explains it with the
same simplicity as Joan of Arc when He says to His Apostles: "He who hears you hears me, and he who rejects you
rejects me, and he who rejects me rejects him who sent me"
(Lk 10:16).

For Christ's Apostles were not merely His subordinates
or His messengers. They were His Body, even His brain
cells. Thus, Saint Paul tells us to have the "mind of Christ"
(Phil 2:5). Unless you are very absentminded or having an
out-of-body experience, you are where your body is. When
I hear your lips speak, I hear *you* speak. When I kiss your
lips, I kiss *you*. When we hear Christ-ordained and Christ-
authorized Apostles, we hear Christ.

And by the authority He gave them when He ordained
them, they gave authority to their successors when they
ordained them. And those successors were from the beginning called bishops, elders, pastors, and presbyters. (Check
it out. It is in the New Testament.) The chain of "apostolic
succession" was never broken, and still exists, visibly. That
is not just a Catholic dogma—it is a historical fact.

The union goes all the way down from Christ to His
Apostles because it goes all the way up from Christ to His
Father. That is why Christ says not only "He who rejects you
rejects me" but also "He who rejects me, rejects him who
sent me." Thus, Christ says that the link between Himself
and His Church is as real as the link between Himself and

His Father. Christ is as really present in the Church as the Father is really present in the Son. Of course, the Church does not reciprocate that presence and love as Christ reciprocates the Father's. She is not perfectly obedient to Him as He is to the Father. But even when she rejects union with Him, He never rejects union with her.

~

To connect this point about the identity of the Church with our previous point about evangelism, there is almost a mathematical formula for it. The Church succeeds in converting the world to the exact extent that she sees and loves and lives her identity with Christ, and fails to the exact extent that she fails to see and love and live that identity and that unity. Did the bishops who blessed anti-Jewish pogroms, did the crusaders who sacked Constantinople, did the priests who lit the fires of the Spanish Inquisition, did the Borgia popes who had bastard children, did the priests who seduced little boys see themselves as Christ's own members, organs, and branches?

What is a saint? A saint is one who actually believes in, and sees (by faith), this mystical union, i.e., the real presence of Christ in all His brothers and sisters, especially the poorest and neediest. A saint is one who really, and not just notionally, understands "As you did it to one of the least of these my brethren, you did it to me" (Mt 25:40). Christ did not say, "I will pretend that you do it to Me"; Christ is not the "great pretender". He did not say, "I legally decree that I will hold you responsible for how you treat those I love as if you were treating Me the same way"; Christ is not a lawyer. He says, as simply and directly and literally and unqualifiedly as it is possible to say in human language, "Whatever you do to them, you are doing to Me."

When Saul, before his conversion, getting his jollies from persecuting Christians, was knocked off his high horse by the light from Heaven on the Damascus road (Acts 9), the voice from Heaven said to him, "Saul, Saul, why do you persecute *me*?" (v. 4; emphasis added). Astonished, Saul asked, "Who are you, Lord?" His whole theology was crumbling. And the reply shocked him even more: "I am Jesus, whom you are persecuting." It was a double shock: first, that Jesus was the Lord God, and second, that Jesus was those men and women Saul was persecuting! These two Persons—Christ's divine Father and Christ's human children—were really so "in" Christ that Christ identified Himself wholly with both of them. Christians are as really "in" Christ, and He in them, as Christ is "in" His Father and His Father "in" Him. That is what Christ Himself says in John 17. Someone once said that if we only understood fully all that the New Testament means when it uses the word "in", we would understand everything that is, from the Trinity to the atom.

So what is the Church, according to Catholic theology? The Church is like a large Eucharist. She is Christ's real presence in the world. To love her is to love Christ; to hate her is to hate Christ.

Though she is an organism, not just an organization, this organism has an organization, as a body has a skeletal structure. And as the soul of an animal is present in all its structured body, giving life to all its structured organs and their acts, so the Spirit of Christ is present in the very structures of the Church as a visible Body, not just in the Church's ethereal ideals.

The order in this "organized religion" is the order of fire, like sparks among reeds: loving authority flashing down and loving obedience flashing up. To see this bonfire of love that is the Church Catholic is to love her; to hate her is not to see her.

32

The Bible

What I want to explore here is not what Protestants can learn from Catholics (e.g., the unscriptural nature of *sola scriptura*) but what Catholics can learn from Protestants, especially about Christocentrism, in dealing with scripture.

How to interpret a religion's scriptures is crucial to every religion because every religion has scriptures (sacred writings), and divisions always appear in the history of a religion over the issue of how to interpret them. All believers accept their scriptures, but not all interpret them the same way. The differences between Protestant and Catholic Christianity center on interpreting the Bible. And both Protestants and Catholics appeal to the Bible to justify their different beliefs about how to interpret the Bible. That fact in itself shows the need for an authoritative interpretation. Every heretic in history has appealed to the Bible.

In Christianity, theology is a science only because of scripture, for a science must have data and scripture is the data for Christian theology. It is the last court of appeal as far as words go, for it is not the word of man but the "Word of God". Differences come in when different interpretations of certain key passage clash, or when different principles of interpretation clash.

Hermeneutics is the science of interpreting a text. Every science has two parts: data and interpretation of the data by hypotheses or theories, which are tested by the data, by how well they explain the data. The source of disagreements in every science is contrary interpretations of the common data; and the source of agreement is in the data themselves, which verify or falsify theories. Interpretations must always be tested by the data, and this is the way to resolve disagreements.

The same is true of theology, which is a science whose data are first of all the Word of God, i.e., divine revelation. If God had not revealed Himself, theology (i.e., supernatural, revealed theology as distinct from natural, philosophical theology) would have no primary data and not be a science. Scripture is to theology what the heavens are to astronomy.

Protestants confine divine revelation to scripture (*sola scriptura*), while Catholics see scripture as only a part, though the most important part, of "Sacred Tradition", which is the actual teaching of the Apostles. This "Sacred Tradition" or "deposit of faith" is frequently appealed to in the New Testament and contrasted with merely human traditions.

But both orthodox Protestants and orthodox Catholics believe in the authority and the infallibility of scripture as divine revelation rather than human speculation. So the most effective key to finding the truth and overcoming errors—and therefore also the most effective key to true unity and agreement about truth—is, for both sides, scripture.

Both sides practice the scientific method in theology in judging theories by data. There are obviously aspects of the scientific method that theology does not use (e.g., mathematical measurement and controlled experiments), but theology uses the basic principle of the scientific method that demands that data judge hypotheses rather than vice versa.

This principle has probably led to more scientific progress than any other. This principle was better understood and obeyed in modern times than in medieval times in every science other than theology. In theology, the reverse is true.

But we must make an important addition: for a Christian, Protestant as well as Catholic, the ultimate datum, the "Word of God", is not merely, or even primarily, scripture, as it is for a Muslim. The Qur'an, not Muhammad, is the heart of Islam. But Christ, not the Bible, is the heart of Christianity. In fact, the primary meaning of the "Word of God" *in the Bible* is not the Bible but Christ. The Bible is its secondary meaning. The Bible is the Word of God on paper, but Christ is the Word of God on wood—the wood of the Cross.

So Christ is the key to interpreting scripture. For He is its point and its unity. Each verse in the Bible is a finger pointing to Him, a dot of paint in His portrait, a cell in His face. Christocentrism applies to scripture too.

So let us see how Christ interprets scripture. Scripture itself gives us some powerful data on this. Let's begin with the example of Christ interpreting scripture to the two disciples on the road to Emmaus, just after His death and Resurrection (Lk 24:13–35). Unless you remember the passage word for word, read it right now before I go any further. If you don't have a Bible, steal one.

If we learn to interpret scripture as Christ did, there will be a "signature" result, the result we find in this passage: our hearts will burn within us as the hearts of the two disciples did. What makes the difference? What made the Gospel the Gospel of the Burning Heart? The answer is simple: Jesus Himself, His presence.

The same is true for us. The presence of the primary "Word of God" (Christ) is the key to interpreting the secondary "Word of God" (scripture).

Saint Augustine's experience is an instructive example. In the *Confessions*, he tells us how when he first read scripture without knowing Christ, he received neither light nor heat from it; but then, later in his life, the second time he read it, he knew Christ, Christ was present to his soul helping him interpret the book; and therefore, he not only loved it for the first time (the heat) but also understood it for the first time (the light).

Why? What was the key to his understanding it and rightly interpreting it? He tells us: he says he "saw one Face".[1] All of scripture's doors then opened to him, once he had the golden key.

Christ is the "face in the picture". Think of those old puzzles for kids where you see a city, or a jungle, and the lines of the buildings or the trees make a hidden face that you have to find. A leaf is an ear, a ladybug is an eye, etc. Once you see the face, you can never again look at the picture without seeing it. Well, the picture is the Bible and the face is Christ. He suddenly pops up out of the pages like a jack-in-the-box. He makes the Bible a pop-up book.

～

Let's look at another passage of scripture that shows us how Jesus interprets scripture.

---

[1] Augustine, *Confessions*, bk. 7, chap. 21, trans. F. J. Sheed, rev. ed. (Indianapolis, Ind.: Hackett, 1993), 124.

And he came to Nazareth, where he had been brought
up; and he went to the synagogue, as was his custom, on
the sabbath day. And he stood up to read; and there was
given to him the book of the prophet Isaiah. He opened
the book and found the place where it was written, "The
Spirit of the Lord is upon me, because he has anointed
me to preach good news to the poor. He has sent me to
proclaim release to the captives and recovering of sight
to the blind, to set at liberty those who are oppressed, to
proclaim the acceptable year of the Lord." And he closed
the book, and gave it back to the attendant, and sat down;
and the eyes of all in the synagogue were fixed on him.
And he began to say to them, "Today this scripture has
been fulfilled in your hearing." (Lk 4:16–21)

Imagine the expectant hush that fell on His hometown
congregation the first time they heard Him preach. Here
was their local hero, already the most famous man in Israel. What would this great rabbi say? Would his wisdom
impress them as much as it had impressed those in other
towns? How would he interpret this passage of scripture?
What new layers of profound rabbinic subtlety would he
show them?

They were shocked to find a different thing altogether.
Instead of a new exegesis of scripture, he was telling them
that they were right now seeing the whole point and meaning and fulfillment of scripture, as the birth of a baby is
the whole point and meaning and fulfillment of a woman's
womb. The Bible is the womb (and so is Mary, and so is
Israel), and Jesus is the baby. Here He is, not merely read
about in the book but outside the book reading it! The congregation was stunned because the Author of the book, and

of the universe, and of themselves, the very Mind of God incarnate, was interpreting His book to them.

He was saying, in effect, "The meaning of this book is something concrete, not something abstract. It is I. I am the meaning of this book, and of its prophecies. I am the way, the way of man to God, because I am the way of God to man. I am the truth, the truth of God, the Mind of God who inspired this book. I am the life, the life of God and the life of this book. I am this book come alive. I am not just your teacher *of* wisdom; I am your wisdom. I am not just your teacher *of* righteousness, and sanctification, and redemption; I am your wisdom and your righteousness and your sanctification and your redemption." His mouthpiece Saint Paul speaks of "Christ Jesus, whom God made our wisdom, our righteousness and sanctification and redemption" (1 Cor 1:30). All these great abstractions—way, truth, life, wisdom, righteousness, sanctification, redemption—are suddenly revealed to be, in their fullness, not abstract but concrete: they are Jesus Himself.

For a thousand years the Jews had faithfully and lovingly read their divinely inspired books as the hands of God, and its prophecies as His pointing fingers. Now the One all the fingers pointed to was here, and it was God Himself, in person. Those who followed the fingers came to Him; those who only looked *at* them rather than looking *along* them did not. Many of them had their nose in the book and would not come to the Author. This was as ironic as if Romeo were to refuse to lift his eyes from the contemplation of Juliet's picture to welcome Juliet herself when she would come knocking at his door and calling, "Romeo, Romeo, where are you, Romeo?" And he would reply, "Go away; I'm looking at my picture of my beloved Juliet. Nothing else matters." This is exactly what Jesus said to them: "You search the Scriptures, because you think that in them you have eternal life; and it is they that bear witness to me; yet you refuse to come to me that you may have life" (Jn 5:39–40).

~

Another passage that exemplifies Jesus' hermeneutics is Luke 20:27–38:

"There came to him some Sadducees, those who say that there is no resurrection" (v. 27). They presented Him with a *reductio ad absurdum* argument, a reduction of the resurrection to an absurdity: if there is a bodily resurrection, whose heavenly wife would a woman be who had legally had seven earthly husbands? After Jesus easily solved the surface problem (we will not "have" each other as exclusive, private spouses in Heaven), He then dug down to the real problem. He proved the reality of the resurrection to the skeptical Sadducees from the only scripture they accepted as divine and infallible, i.e., the Pentateuch, the first five books of Moses: "But that the dead are raised, even Moses showed, in the passage about the bush [Ex 3], where he calls the Lord the God of Abraham and the God of Isaac and the God of Jacob. Now he is not God of the dead, but of the living; for all live to him" (vv. 37–38).

Christ refuted the skeptics from their own scriptures by bringing together, like match, kindling, and fuel, three of their scriptures' divinely revealed names for God: (1) the God of Abraham, Isaac, and Jacob; (2) the God of the living, not of the dead; and (3) God's own self-revealed name, spoken to Moses in the burning bush (Ex 3:14), the name that was so holy that no Jew ever would pronounce it: I AM

(JHWH). It can mean "I am what I am" or "I will be what I will be" but not "I was what I was." It is the name of the living present and the to-be-born future, not of the dead past.

I AM was present to Moses 430 years after Abraham died, and yet He called Himself the God of Abraham. He says not "I *was* the God of Abraham" but "I AM the God of Abraham"—because Abraham and everyone else in time "live to him", live in His presence. For us, the past is dead and the dead are gone, but not to God. For this God, unlike the gods of the pagans, is the God of all life, not the god of death, the god of corpses. That would be a demon or an idol.

The logic is stunning and simple: if He still said, "I AM the God of Abraham" 430 years after Abraham died, and if He is not the god of the dead but the God of the living, then Abraham must now be living in His presence, and in His present, not His past. And Abraham is no freak, no exception. There must be for us too a resurrection from the dead, because we will still live to God, and God has no dead past, only the living present.

Notice the four profoundly connected meanings of the word "present". It means (1) the live present moment, not the dead past; (2) being here rather than there, present rather than absent and far away; (3) "being-with" someone, aware of that someone, face-to-face with that someone—not *absent-minded*; and (4) *a* present, a gift given rather than withheld, most of all the gift of yourself to another self. "Present" is the opposite of (1) past, (2) absent, (3) unknown, and (4) withheld. Meditate on this connection.

So Jesus is saying to the skeptical Sadducees that the ultimate reason for the resurrection is the nature of God as eternally present to us, presenting Himself as His Christmas present to us, His love-gift. In other words, man is resurrected because God is love, and love is alive and present and stronger than death.

Because God is the inventor of life and is the source of all the energy of life, when He is present the dead come to life, just as when fire is present to things, things get burned. Dead people came back to life at least three times that we know of: see the accounts of Lazarus (Jn 11), the widow's son at Nain (Lk 7), and Jairus' daughter (Mk 5). As vampires cannot survive the sunlight, death cannot survive the Sonlight.

And therefore we are resurrected too, if He is our God and we are His children. There is an "if" because presence is reciprocal: I am not present to you if you notice me but I do not notice you, or vice versa. It takes two to tango, and two to be present. The reason God made each of us an *I* is so that we and God could make ourselves into a *we*—like God Himself, who is a *we*, a Trinity.

The Sadducees' deeper mistake was not that they did not know the resurrection—that was just a symptom—but that they did not know God, they did not know the "face in the picture". They had their nose in the book, even when its Author and main character was right in front of their noses. They were like Job's three friends, who said pious things *about* God as if He were absent. They should have been like Job, who said much less pious things but addressed them *to* the God who was present. That is what Jesus gives us: the real presence of God. The One who refuted the Sadducees by *interpreting* the supremely sacred word in scripture that

Moses heard from the burning bush was the One who had *spoken* those words in the burning bush! He was interpreting His own words. This man was God.

~

But (we may ask with Nicodemus) how can such things be? How can man and God become one? How can the infinite gap between Creator and creature be crossed?

It can be done not by the creature but only by the Creator. The creature can no more become the Creator than a character in a book can become the author. But the author can become a character without ceasing to be the author. Alfred Hitchcock and M. Night Shyamalan did it in their movies. They put themselves into them without ceasing to be the transcendent creators of them. Thus, the Creator can become a creature without ceasing to be the Creator, as Hitchcock and Shyamalan became movie actors without ceasing to be moviemakers. Transcendence can include immanence.

And this is why we can meet God: only because of Christ. He says so Himself: "No one has ever seen God; the only-begotten Son, who is in the bosom of the Father, he has made him known" (Jn 1:18). We can't go up and bring Him down, but He can come down and bring us up.

~

Here is Jesus' single most practical and important principle of hermeneutics: "My teaching is not mine, but his who sent me; if any man's will is to do his will, he shall know whether the teaching is from God" (Jn 7:16–17).

We've seen that only by knowing God can we properly interpret His words in scripture, just as only by knowing Romeo can Juliet properly interpret his love letters. And since love is essentially an act of will, the most important principle of hermeneutics is to will God's will, i.e., to love God, i.e., to be a saint. Only if our heart (which means primarily the will) is "online" with God, will our mind be. The cause of our minds being aligned is our wills being aligned, not vice versa. The will teaches the mind here. We think the intellect is always the soul's navigator, while the will is its captain. But here, the will is the navigator too. For "the heart has reasons which the reason does not know" (Pascal). The heart has eyes. Love has eyes. Love is not blind. How could love be blind?—God is love. Is God blind?

Many theologians give the impression that they have never learned this simple Lesson One, the thing that every child knows about God: that He is a Person. Theologians typically treat hermeneutics as an impersonal science, like linguistics. That is like interpreting a love letter by correcting its grammar. It is highly insulting to the lover.

The Sadducees were uncomprehending because they were unbelieving, not vice versa. Their minds were clouded because their wills were divided. Religious belief is not first of all an intellectual opinion but an act of will, a personal trust. The Sadducees' minds were not clear because their hearts were not pure. "Purity of heart is to will one thing", says Kierkegaard, and that one thing is God's will. That is why saints make the best scripture scholars. That is why Mother Teresa's simple words carried more weight than tons of tomes. Once, she was persuaded to listen to a day of papers by scholarly theologians and afterward was asked her opinion about them. "I think they talk too much", she said.

"But Mother, that's their job. What else could they have done?" "Well, this room's pretty dusty. If one of them had picked up a broom and used it, I think that would have said a lot more."

The Word of God says that "the Word of God is living and active, sharper than any two-edged sword, piercing to the division of soul and spirit, of joints and marrow" (Heb 4:12). If we are saints, that sword pierces our heart and draws blood. To be a saint is to fall on that sword and die to yourself. That is the only right suicide, and the only right hermeneutics.

And only when both Protestants and Catholics see the distinction between saints and scholars as more important than the distinction between Protestants and Catholics will they come together in interpreting their common Bible.

33

The Catholic Jesus versus
the Protestant Jesus

This short note is written to my Catholic brothers and sisters, not to my Protestant ones.

There is no difference in theology between these two Jesuses, because the theology of the Protestant Jesus is borrowed from the councils and creeds of the Catholic Church. But there is a difference in the psychology. The typically Protestant Jesus is nice; the typically Catholic Jesus is formidable.

I'm dealing with unfair stereotypes here, idealizing the "Catholic Jesus" and satirizing the "Protestant Jesus". Many Catholics believe in the "Protestant Jesus", and many Protestants believe in the "Catholic Jesus". My point here is not Catholic apologetics but Christian iconography. I don't claim that all Protestants buy into the Protestant Jesus, any more than I claim that all Catholics buy into the Catholic Jesus. But if you look at the actual writings of the Catholic saints and spiritual writers, you never forget the divinity, even while you focus on the humanity. The Catholic Jesus is to be adored, to be worshipped, with awe and wonder. He is the great "*Lion* of the tribe of Judah" (Rev 5:5; emphasis added). He is Aslan. The Protestant Jesus (especially the version in many parachurches) is a pussycat. He is embarrassingly a human projection. He is dangerously close to Ned Flanders from *The Simpsons*.

So when this book calls for Catholics to learn from their Protestant Evangelical friends about the centrality of Christ and personal intimacy with Him, I most certainly do not mean that.

34

The Bottom Line

The bottom line is Christ. A Catholic justifies his Catholicism by the very same ultimate allegiance as a Protestant justifies his Protestantism. The only justifiable motive for a Catholic to remain a Catholic or for a Protestant to become one is that that is Christ's will. The only justifiable motive for a Protestant to remain a Protestant or for a Catholic to become one is that that is Christ's will.

The difference, then, is not ontological. It is the same Christ. The difference is theological. It is a different theory or belief or theology or ecclesiology about Christ: Does He have a visible "mystical body" that is the Catholic Church, which He authored and authorized to teach and sanctify in His name? The essential Protestant claim is that Catholics have added their barnacles to the simple Gospel, which is "Jesus only". The essential Catholic claim is that Protestants have chopped branches off the tree which is the full Christ, Head and Body (Church).

Do Catholics forget their first love? Do Catholics forget the point Protestants remember, i.e., "Jesus only"? Many Catholics do, like my students at Boston College. But they are not doctors of the Church, or saints, or mystics. Saint Thomas Aquinas is all three. Shortly before Saint

Thomas' death, Christ spoke to him from a crucifix (according to sworn testimony from Thomas' friend and confessor, Brother Reginald) and said, "You have written well about Me, Thomas. What will you have as your reward?" And Thomas' reply, which was his final word to his Lord, was: "Only Yourself, Lord". For him, as for the Apostles after the Transfiguration, it was "Jesus only".

That is exactly the main and central and essential and best point of Protestantism.

Saint Thomas' favorite theologian was Saint Augustine. Saint Augustine said, in the *Confessions*, "Surely a man is unhappy even if he knows all these things but does not know You; and that man is happy who knows You even though he knows nothing of them. And the man who knows both You and them is not the happier for them but only on account of You."[1] That is exactly what Saint Thomas said, in fewer words and with less eloquence.

The "only" part of "Jesus only" or "Only Yourself, Lord" is the hard part for us to believe and live. But those who believe it and live it are saints. That is the source of their joy and their lightness. That is why they can joke with life itself on their deathbeds or as they are being martyred. As Chesterton says, in his poem "Ecclesiastes", "One thing alone is needful: everything. The rest is vanity of vanities." Jesus is everything.

"Jesus only" is not reductionism. Reductionism is one of the worst of all intellectual errors. It reduces more to less, great to small, valid to invalid, substance to accident, whole to parts, eternity to time, person to thing, absolute to

---

[1] Augustine, *Confessions*, bk. 5, chap. 4, trans. F. J. Sheed (Indianapolis, Ind.: Hackett, 1993), 72.

relative. Whenever we hear the word "only", which is the one-word formula for all reductionism, a bell of suspicion should instantly go off in our mind. The only "only" that is not reductionism is "Jesus only". Because Jesus is all. "Jesus only" means "reality only, goodness only, God's will only, eternal divine love only".

Every other "only" excludes something. Jesus excludes nothing. The full Christ is Head and Body, God and man, Creator and creature. Even "God the Father" excludes creatures: the Father is not any creature, and no creature is the Father. But Christ is both Creator and creature, divine and human, eternal and temporal. This simple center is the whole circle. This "Protestant point" is precisely the Catholic point, for "catholic" means "universal".

When the two beams of the Cross crossed, it was at a single point. That point was the center of the circle of everything. That was the still point of the turning world. But those two beams, unlike the circle of Buddhism, extend out infinitely in all four directions of the compass, and encompass everything.

Wise and holy Catholics like Saint Thomas see this simple Christ, this positive "Protestant point", at the heart of their religion. If all Catholics do that, and if Protestants see that they do that, Protestants will come home. If not, not.

Conclusion

I probably surprised you by how short my introduction was. My conclusion will be even shorter. I do not draw any conclusions. That would be what Tolkien's Ents would call "too hasty". It is too early in the day, too early in the ecumenical era, to prophesy.

But it is not too early to begin. Instead of concluding with claims about how ecumenical reunion will end, I will conclude with a claim about how it must begin.

It must begin in our hearts, with our *passionate* love of Christ and therefore of His will that His children become one. He will honor that desire in proportion to its temperature.

But His Church will become wholly whole when it becomes wholly holy. The most immediate reason we are not yet one is that you and I are not yet saints. Only the fire of saintly love is hot enough to fuse us together.

And that is something every single one of us can do something about, immediately, if not sooner.

There is no easier way to do it. I am truly sorry that there is no easier way to do it. The easiest things to understand are usually the hardest things to do—like the Ten Commandments. To avoid doing them, we pretend we don't understand them. We are comforted by our skepticisms, for even though all forms of skepticism are logically self-contradictory (is it true that there is no truth?), they are morally very comforting and convenient. They absolve us of responsibility for doing what we pretend we don't understand. But it is a lie. We do understand. Deep down, you already knew everything I said in this book.

So what are you going to do about that?